Guided Reading Management

Structure and Organization

for the Classroom

Grades 1-4

Guided Reading Management

Structure and Organization for the Classroom (1-4)

by
Patricia Pavelka

Edited by
Lois Schenking

Cover and Illustrations by
Patrick Vincent

Husky Trail Press LLC
East Lyme, CT

Husky Trail Press LLC
PO Box 705
East Lyme, CT 06333
860-739-7644
888-775-5211
860-691-8066 fax
www.huskytrailpress.com
info@huskytrailpress.com

Editor: Lois Schenking
Cover and Illustrations: Patrick Vincent

ISBN No. 978-1-935258-04-9

Library of Congress Catalog Number

DEDICATION

To Pat Terry and Pam Terry, you were with me when the first edition was published seven years ago and we continue to spend treasured times together. You always demonstrate that anything is possible as long as we have faith, family, and friends. Thank you for your endless support and love.

I offer a heartfelt thank you to all of the teachers who have written, e-mailed, phoned, and shared their students' amazing work. It has been such a privilege to be included in your educational walk.

ACKNOWLEDGEMENTS

Thank you to

Mom, my role model for life.

Lois Schenking, my editor. You always roll up your sleeves, find the smallest details, and dig in through the wee hours of the night.

Jo-Ann Geida. Your journey with me has included everything from scanning hundreds and hundreds of student samples, to road trips, to making ten visits a day from your office to mine, to …

Patrick Vincent. Your artistic abilities are incredible. Anything from a serious picture, to a line drawing, to pictures that make us laugh out loud. Just love the book's new mascot.

Sharon Smith. Your interest and support is greatly appreciated. Your ideas for the cover look great.

Dana LaPorta. You take my ideas and bring them to life in your classroom.

Lorraine Walker. Fifteen years ago you believed in me and published my first book. You will always hold a special place in my heart.

Sumner County Educators in Tennessee who are far too numerous to name. You have welcomed me with open arms into your district and schools. Your willingness to try new things and share ideas is greatly treasured. The dedication and enthusiasm of the reading coaches has been an inspiration to me and I look forward to our Fridays together.

Emily Kresse. You are a creative artist, writer, and student.

Souring Heights Charter School Educators in New Jersey. You've invited me to teach with you, work with your students, exchange ideas, take pictures, and share students' work. Stephanie Mastropaolo, Hilary Bowden, Lisa Dinallo, Barbara McGrath, Hilary Battes, Karissa Patrisso, Samantha Berman, Joan Incognito, Joanna D'Auria and Stacy Vetter; it is an honor to be a part of your classrooms. Thank you Claudia Zuorick and Jackie Quagliana for all the planning to bring me to your school.

Richard LaPorta. It still amazes me how you can take pages of a word document and turn it into a book. You are and will always be my number one fan and big brother.

TABLE OF CONTENTS

Part 1
Organizing and Scheduling
Guided Reading Groups

Part 2
What Are the Other Students Doing
While I Am with a Guided Reading Group?

Part 3
Putting It All Together

Part 4
Appendix

INTRODUCTION

The first edition of *Guided Reading Management: Structure and Organization for the Classroom* was written seven years ago. Since then I have researched and worked with educators and students across the country to refine what can be, and is often thought of, a complicated system. This second edition clarifies and simplifies guided reading management. New explanations, samples, centers, and rotation options are included. These will help your classrooms be highly organized and effective. This book takes you through the steps needed for a successful guided reading program.

In working with educators, a common theme is repeated again and again: it is not the instruction that teachers are having difficulty with, it is the management.

How many groups a day can I realistically take?

How do I structure my classroom?

What are the other kids doing?

My students cannot work independently.

I'm always interrupted while working with guided reading groups.

Giving directions takes too long. It's cutting into my group time.

There are many resources available for teachers in the area of reading instruction (including at the end of this book). However, there are limited resources available for teachers to get help with the management piece.

The purpose of this book is to help teachers with the structure and management of their classrooms during guided reading instruction. This is not a theory book, nor is it a book about guided reading instruction. *Guided Reading Management: Structure and Organization for the Classroom* will show you specific easy-to-implement structures, strategies, ideas, and activities to put all of the components of managing Guided Reading together successfully. This book is an "I can do it tomorrow" kind of resource. Suggestions read about today can be implemented in classrooms tomorrow.

There are three things happening during small group instruction time. This book discusses these three components. Below is a visual overview depicting the components.

1
The teacher is working with a small guided reading group

4-6 students

3
The remaining students are working on independent work

2
There is a background group meeting on the floor to the left or right of the teacher

4-6 students

This book is divided into four parts.

Part 1
Organizing and Scheduling the Groups

This part shows very specific ways to organize and schedule 4 or 5 guided reading groups. There are a variety of different schedules from which to choose depending upon your specific classroom needs. This section also describes background groups. Background groups are guided reading groups that are not meeting with the teacher on that particular day. Background groups may be working with book boxes or literature discussion boxes. These are described in detail.

Part 2
What are the other students doing while the teacher is with a guided reading group?

This part gives a wealth of assignments and activities that students can be working with while the teacher is instructing a guided reading group. These assignments are multi-leveled so that struggling learners as well as proficient learners will benefit from them. The assignments are organized into five different categories:

Writing Activities
Literature Connections
Language Arts
Sight Vocabulary
Additional Activities

These assignments are presented in a way that shows how they can be utilized as learning centers or as independent seat work. The suggested assignments can be coordinated with your curriculum and books.

Part 3
Putting It All Together

This part shows how to coordinate guided reading groups with work groups. It shows how to use a rotation wheel to move students from one assignment to another. This part also shows how to get started step-by-step. There is a schedule for the first four to five weeks of implementing the ideas, activities, and strategies in this book.

Part 4
Appendix

This part provides reproducibles of activities and strategies discussed. These may be copied and used immediately in classrooms. Also provided is a bibliography of educational resources: professional books, children's books, and other materials.

Part 1

Organizing and Scheduling Guided Reading Groups

ORGANIZING AND SCHEDULING GROUPS

One of the most difficult tasks when implementing guided reading is the management piece. How many groups a day will I take? What will my schedule look like? Do I take all groups every day? This section will address these questions and more.

The following scenarios for organizing and scheduling guided reading groups will take approximately one hour each day. So you would provide 60 minutes of small guided reading group instruction per day. Anything over that hour is usually spent in whole group situations.

A one-hour block can be divided into approximately three twenty-minute segments. During that hour block, students would spend:

twenty minutes at one center,

twenty minutes at a second center, and

twenty minutes in a small group, either guided reading with the teacher or in a background group. (Background groups are explained on pages 25-55)

This is a general idea for time frames. Realistically, if you only have exactly one hour for small groups instruction, your groups would run for fifteen minutes each, not twenty, because transition time is needed between each group. Also you could schedule your three time frames so that you meet with one group for a longer period of time.

ORGANIZING AND SCHEDULING FIVE GUIDED READING GROUPS

To the right is a schedule for working with five groups. Each of the five guided reading groups is represented by squares. Groups should be limited to no more than six students.

ORGANIZING AND SCHEDULING
FIVE GUIDED READING GROUPS

Monday	Tuesday	Wednesday	Thursday	Friday

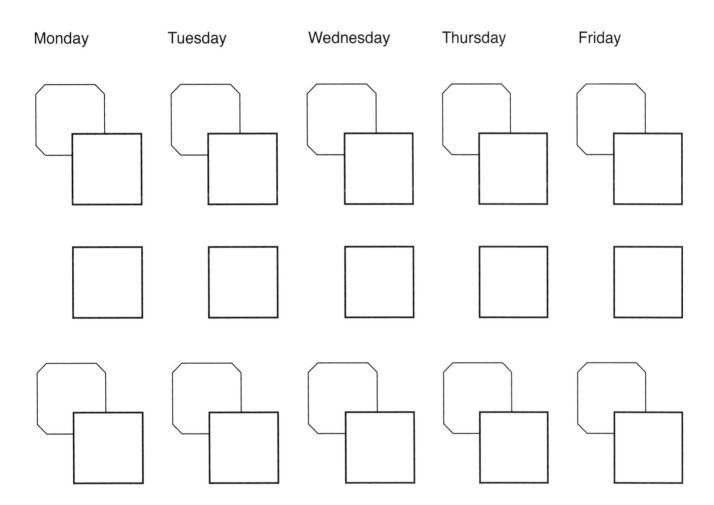

The guided reading groups are leveled so that you have groups of students who are working at their instructional levels. The five groups will show a range of reading abilities. The guided reading group is shown by the dark bordered square. The background group is shown by the lighter rounded square in the back.

Group A is the neediest group of students. These are your most fragile readers who need a lot of support and instruction. These are students who may have reading difficulties. These are students the teacher is most concerned about.

Group E is your most proficient group of readers. These are students who are either learning the reading process very quickly and easily or are fluent readers.

Groups B, C, and D are in corresponding order of their instructional levels. B is the second "neediest" group while D is the second "highest" group. C is the median group.

You want to take group A every day. These are students who need as much support in their reading development as possible. In the diagram on the following page, they are the center group.

You now have four groups left. Pair a less-abled group with a more independent group. You could pair up the four remaining groups the following ways:

> Group B and Group D   Group C and Group E

OR

> Group B and Group E   Group C and Group D

For the following example, we will pair groups B & E together and groups C & D together.

Groups B and E are always called to meet at the same time. One group works with the teacher in a guided reading group while the other group is the background group. Remember, the dark front square represents the group that will be working with the teacher in guided reading. The lighter rounded square represents the background group. The background group will meet to the left or right of the guided reading group and work with reading boxes or literature discussion boxes. (These boxes and the organization of the background groups are explained in detail starting on page 25).

Each day groups B and E reverse places. See the diagram below.

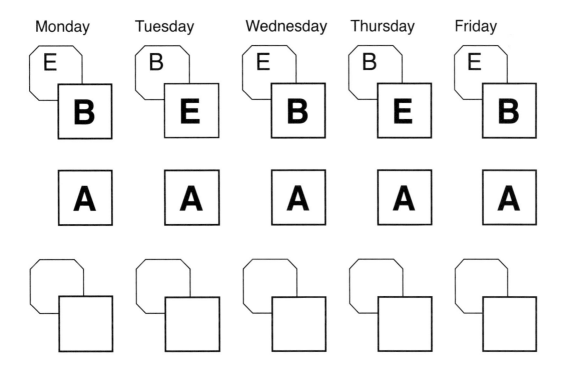

Groups C and D are always called to meet at the same time. One group works with the teacher in a guided reading group while the other group is the background group. Each day groups C and D reverse places. See the diagram below.

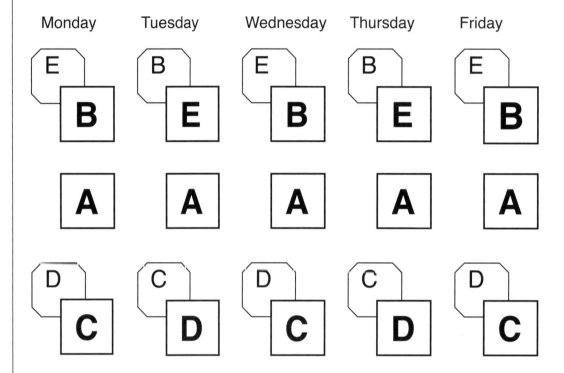

You work with your neediest readers five days a week (A), your developing readers three days a week (B&C), and your independent readers two days a week (D&E).

Let's look at Monday in detail

Monday

20 minutes

E
B

First 20 minutes
B is the guided reading group.
E is the background group.
A, C, D are at centers.

20 minutes

A

Second 20 minutes
A is the guided reading group.
There is no background group.
B, C, D, & E are at centers.

20 minutes

D
C

Third 20 minutes
C is the guided reading group.
D is the background group.
A, B & E are at centers.

Let's look at the Week in detail

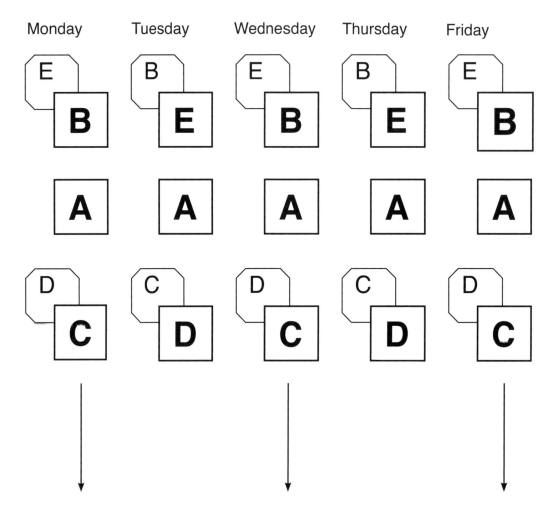

On Monday, Wednesday, and Friday, the teacher meets with groups B, A, and then C, for 20 minute guided reading lessons each. Groups E and D work as background groups.

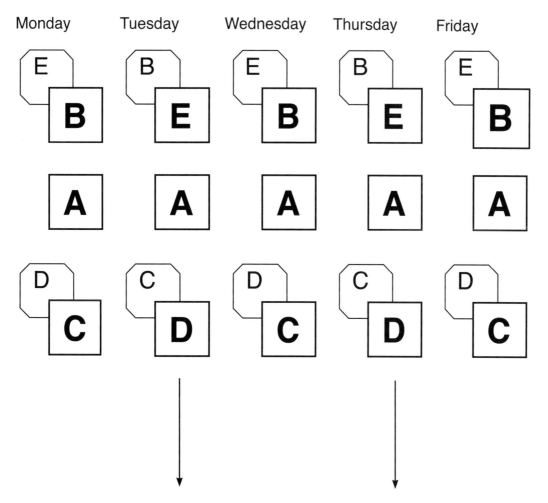

Monday	Tuesday	Wednesday	Thursday	Friday
E B	B E	E B	B E	E B
A	A	A	A	A
D C	C D	D C	C D	D C

On Tuesday and Thursday, the teacher meets with groups E, A, and then D, for 20 minute guided reading lessons each. Groups B and C work as background groups.

Now that you have your basic weekly schedule organized, you want to make it flexible, depending on the needs of your students. We will create a two-cycle schedule. On the following pages are some options from which to choose. Each option is a two-week cycle.

Option 1

This is an option for classrooms that have one significantly below grade level group. Notice that A is always in the middle. They always meet 5 days. You will start with a different group of the paired groups each Monday. So, if in week one you started on Monday morning with group B and group E was your background group, then the next week you would start with group E on Monday morning and group B would be your background group.

Weekly Schedule 1 (Weeks 1, 3, 5, 7, 9, etc.)

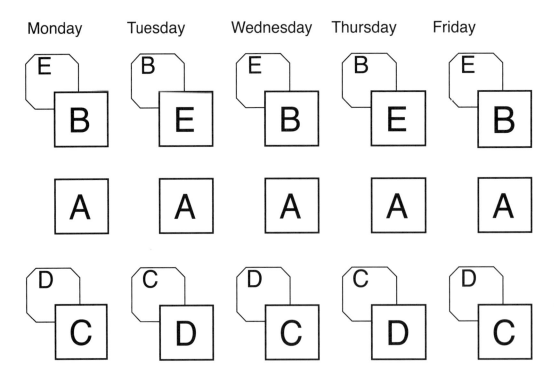

This week groups B & C meet with the teacher three times. Groups D & E meet with the teacher two times. Group A meets with the teacher every day.

Option 1 (continued)

Weekly Schedule 2 (Weeks 2, 4, 6, 8, 10, etc.)

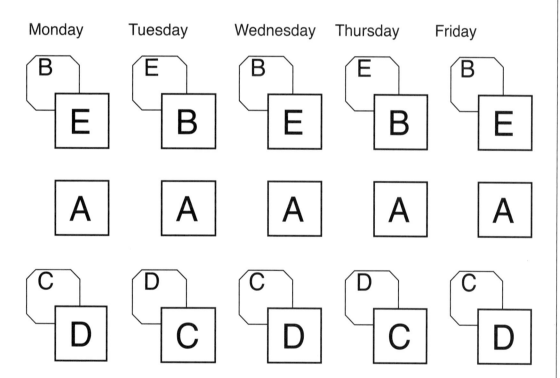

This week groups D & E meet with the teacher three times. Groups B & C meet with the teacher two times. Group A meets with the teacher every day.

Option 2
This is an option for classrooms that have two groups of struggling readers. If there are two groups of students that you are concerned about (groups A and B), then have them reverse places each week.

Weekly Schedule 1 (Weeks 1, 3, 5, 7, 9, etc.)

This week Group A works with the teacher in a guided reading format five days. Group B works with the teacher in a guided reading format three days.

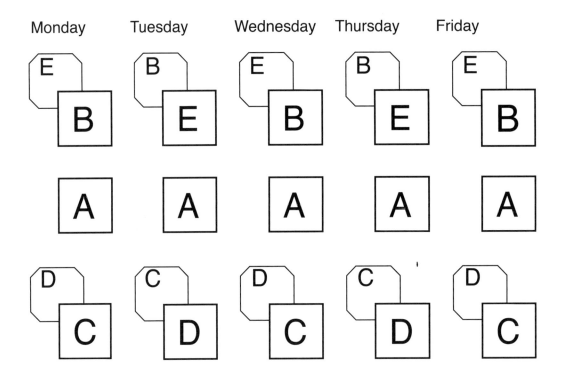

This week Group C works with the teacher three times. Groups D & E work with the teacher two times.

Option 2 (continued)

Weekly Schedule 2 (Weeks 2, 4, 6, 8, 10, etc.)

This week Group B works with the teacher in a guided reading format five days. Group A works with the teacher in a guided reading format three days.

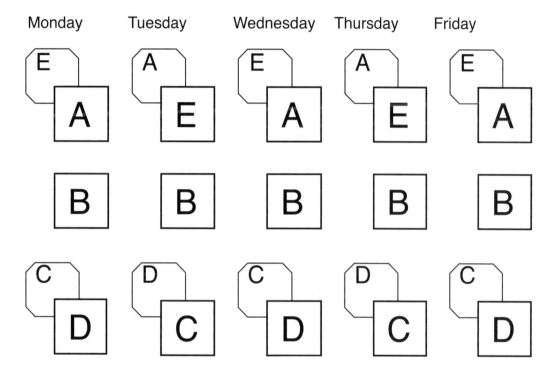

This week Group D works with the teacher three times. Groups C and E work with the teacher two times. In this option you work with your weakest groups five days, then three days, five days, then three days.

In the Appendix is a blank reproducible of these scheduling boxes. I used a two-week cycle for my guided reading groups. The first two pages of my plan book were these scheduling sheets. I always knew which groups I was taking without having to search and rewrite the schedule each week.

ORGANIZING AND SCHEDULING
FOUR GUIDED READING GROUPS

Following is a schedule for working with four groups. Each of the four guided reading groups is represented by a square. The four groups will show a range of reading abilities. You will use the following scale:

Group A is the neediest group of students. These are your most fragile readers who need a lot of support and instruction. These are students who may have reading difficulties.

Group B is the next neediest group of students. These are students who would also greatly benefit from working every day with the teacher.

Group C has students who are approximately at grade level.

Group D is your most proficient group of readers. These are students who are either learning the reading process very quickly and easily or are fluent readers.

You want to take groups A and B every day. These are students who need as much support in their reading development as possible. The following diagram shows groups A and B meeting with the teacher daily for guided reading.

ORGANIZING AND SCHEDULING
FOUR GUIDED READING GROUPS

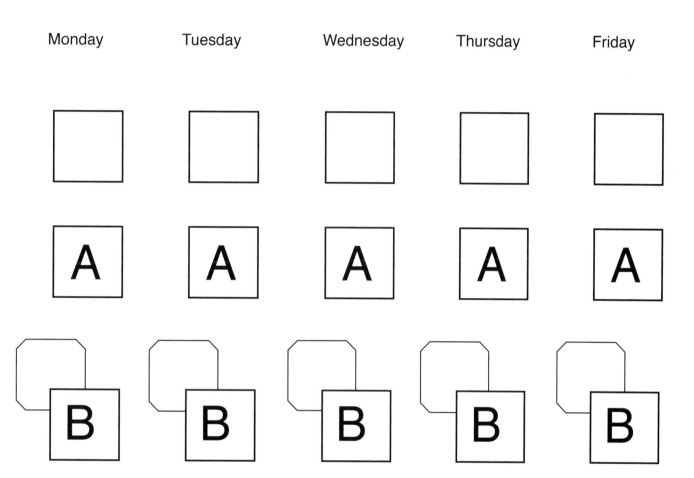

You now have two groups left, C and D. Groups C and D are taken every other day for guided reading. While one group works with the teacher in guided reading, the other group is a background group.

The front, dark bordered square is the group that will be working with the teacher in guided reading. The back, lighter rounded square represents the background group. The background group will meet to the left or right of the guided reading group and work with reading boxes or literature discussion boxes. (These boxes and the organization of the background groups are explained in detail starting on page 25). Below is a two-week cycle schedule.

Weekly Schedule 1

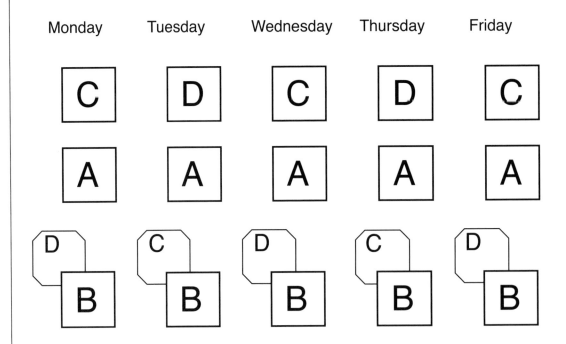

This week groups A and B work with the teacher in a guided reading format all five days. Group C works with the teacher three days and group D works with the teacher two days in a guided reading format.

Weekly Schedule 2

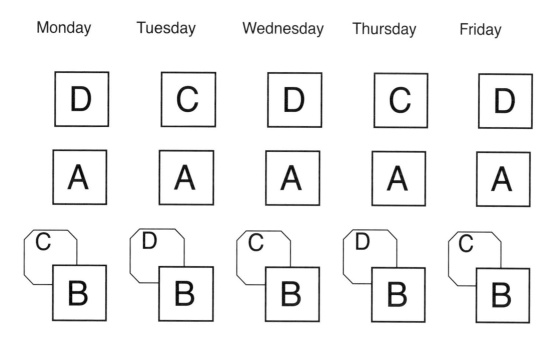

This week groups A and B work with the teacher in a guided reading format all five days. Group D works with the teacher three days and group C works with the teacher two days in a guided reading format.

ORGANIZING AND SCHEDULING FOUR GUIDED READING GROUPS WITH WHOLE GROUP INSTRUCTION

Some teachers have expressed frustration in trying to schedule small guided reading groups as well as work in their basal with the whole class. The following schedules try to provide time for both.

Using a four-group model, in the following schedule, no groups would be taken on Monday. Instead the time would be used for whole class instruction and discussions of new concepts and skills for the week and/or introducing a new story in the basal.

On Tuesday, you would meet with groups B, A, then C. Group D would be a background group during the first twenty minutes.

On Wednesday, you would meet with groups D, A, then B. Group C would be a background group during the last twenty minutes.

On Thursday, you would meet with groups B, A, then C. Group D would be a background group during the first twenty minutes.

On Friday, only the weakest group would meet with you and the rest of the period would be spent in a whole group format.

In summary:
Group A meets in a small group with you four days a week.
Group B meets in a small group with you three days a week.
Group C meets in a small group with you two days a week and one day in a
      background group.
Group D meets in a small group with you one day a week and two days in a
      background group.

ORGANIZING AND SCHEDULING
FOUR GUIDED READING GROUPS
WITH WHOLE GROUP INSTRUCTION

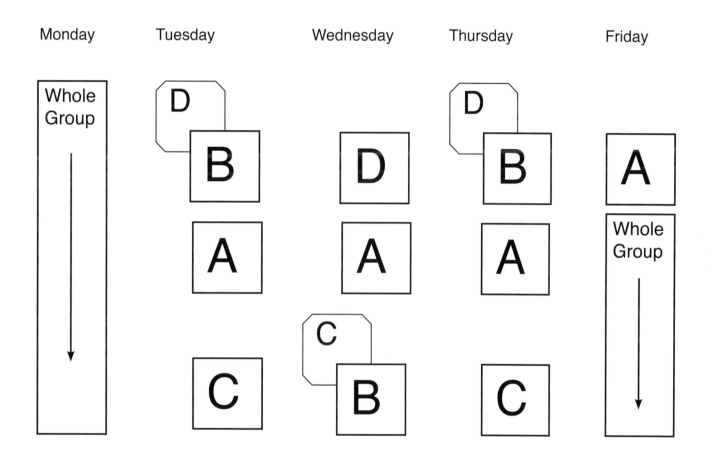

Another option is to work whole class with the basal on Mondays and Fridays and work with small groups on Tuesday, Wednesday and Thursday. See the example.

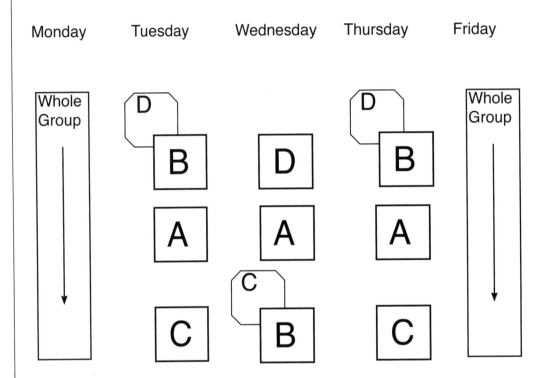

In the above example:

Group A meets in a small group with you three days a week.

Group B meets in a small group with you three days a week.

Group C meets in a small group with you two days a week and one day in a background group.

Group D meets in a small group with you one day a week and two days in a background group.

There are so many ways to schedule and organize the groups. This section gives you only a small sampling of ideas. In the appendix is a blank reproducible for each of the scheduling options described. Take the blank reproducibles, copy them, and lay two pages out in front of you. Now think about your students and their groups. Start filling in the boxes as you think of the following questions:

How many groups do I have?
How many weaker versus stronger groups do I have?
Who do I want to take most often?
How much whole group time do I need?
How many days a week will I meet with small groups

After you have filled in the boxes, look at your two-week cycle. Ask yourself the above questions again and make revisions. I actually enlarged the boxes and used them as my plan book. You can write your actual plans in the boxes and it's very visual. It shows the groups you are taking today; the order you are taking them; and what your plans are for the day. It also shows you who is in the background group. The first two pages of my planbook were these scheduling sheets. I always knew which groups I was taking without having to search and rewrite the schedule each week.

MAKING GUIDED READING GROUPS FLEXIBLE

Each student is a member of a reading group that is at his/her instructional level. When these groups meet, it is either with the teacher in a guided reading format or in a background group working with reading boxes or literature discussion boxes.

The guided reading groups are flexible. Groups are changed approximately every four to six weeks depending upon your assessments and the students' needs. There may be only a small amount of movement. You do not need to change all of the group's membership. The changes are subtle.

Students may move to a group working with easier books or more challenging books, depending upon their needs. For example, if a student is having difficulty with fluency, move him/her to a group working with easier texts so fluency can be addressed. After the four weeks, you may move him/her back to his/her original level to see if there are improvements.

By moving just one or two students, the whole group dynamic changes! Groups do not become stagnant with the same students always working together. Each group has a least one new member who brings new ideas and personality.

Students need to see that you are moving them around to all different levels depending upon their needs at the time. Sometimes they will be working with easier texts. Sometimes they will be working with harder texts. When students see that groups are flexible and not the same for months on end, they lose that sense of "top group" and "bottom group" labels.

Each time new guided reading groups are formed, students give themselves a name based on a science or social studies theme being studied at that time. Below is a picture showing reading boxes (explained on pages 25-40) titled with names based on a science unit about the ocean.

Calling groups by letters or numbers such as A,B,C, etc. or 1,2,3, etc. seems to make students more aware of levels. Even when arbitrarily assigning letters or numbers to groups, some students appear to be concerned about the levels. Letters are used in Part 1 of this book to explain the group rotations to make it easier for you to understand, but in the classroom with the students, different titles are used.

 **Skiers**

Snowmen

One classroom based their group's names on the winter season

 **Skaters**

Evergreens

BACKGROUND GROUPS

A background group is a group of students who work together to the left or right of the guided reading group that is meeting with the teacher. This group is, in reality, a guided reading group that is not meeting with the teacher but working independently next to him/her.

Background groups are used for a number of reasons. The first reason is for "crowd control." If your class size is 25 students and you call five students to work with you, there are 20 other students "out there" working alone. If you can get another 5 or 6 out of the "mainstream," it makes a big difference! Instead of five students working with you, there will be 11 students working either with or near you.

The background group is much more "on task" with its assignments because of the close proximity to you. You can give the same assignment to those out there in the "mainstream," but they probably will not be on task as much as when they have been called up by you and are working close to you. There are also fewer distractions when they are working as a background group.

> The background groups are working with one of two things:
>
> reading boxes (described on the following pages)
> or
> literature discussion boxes (beginning on page 41)

READING BOXES

Reading boxes are used by emergent readers, beginning readers, and struggling readers. These readers need to read short, familiar stories and texts over and over again to increase fluency, build sight vocabulary, and increase comprehension.

Reading boxes are also used by fluent readers who are not comfortable with or motivated to read long books/novels.

Quick Overview of Reading Boxes

What are reading boxes?

Reading boxes are boxes or plastic tubs of reading materials created especially for each guided reading group to use when it is meeting as a background group.

How are the reading boxes organized?

The reading materials in the boxes are leveled to be as perfect a match as possible for each group of students. Materials are at students' independent reading levels.

Who uses reading boxes?

The background groups use their designated reading boxes.

When are reading boxes used?

Reading boxes are used by a background group while the teacher is working with a guided reading group.

Where are reading boxes used?

Reading boxes are used on the floor located directly to the right or left of the teacher and his/her guided reading group.

Why are reading boxes created and used?

Students are reading silently at their independent levels. They are practicing, utilizing, and applying reading strategies.

Preparation For Reading Boxes

Preparation of the Classroom
Colored Sitting Circles

Make six large different colored circles using 9x12 oaktag. Laminate the circles to make them more durable. Tape them on the floor as shown in the diagram below. These circles will help students find their places quickly when they are called to meet as a background group. Students can sit on any color they wish or they may be assigned a color by the teacher. Different colored mats or carpet squares also work well.

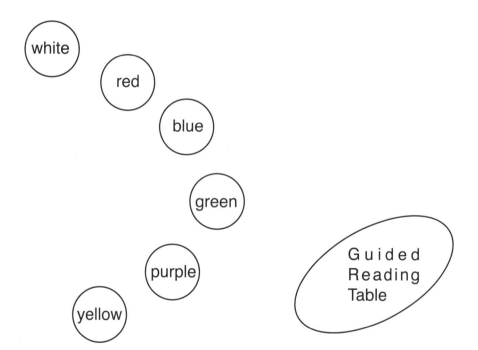

Front of Reading Boxes

Put an index card or piece of paper on the front of each reading box. Write the names of students in the group that will be using that particular box for reading.

Put a clothespin next to a name. This student is the Reader of the Day. Each time the background group meets and works with its reading box, the clothespin gets moved to the next person. Each child gets a turn to be the Reader of the Day. The Reader of the Day is explained on pages 35-36.

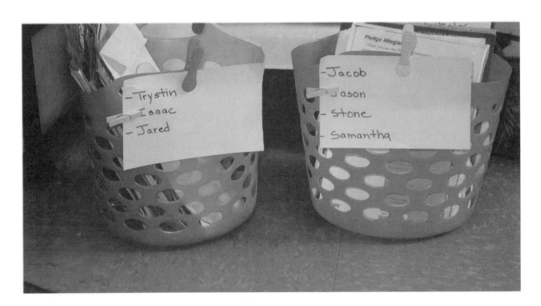

Back of Reading Boxes

Laminate three blank 5x7 index cards for each reading box. Put the three cards on the back side of each reading box. These cards will be used for activities to make the reading boxes manipulative for students (explained on pages 38-40).

Colored Circle Cards

Using 5x7 index cards, make a set of cards for each reading box with colored circles that match the colored circles or mats placed on the floor (see page 27).

Highlighter Tape Cards

Highlighter tape is tape that is reusable and comes in fluorescent colors. Students can put it on and take it off pages of books.

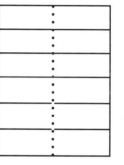

You need three pieces of 9x12 white construction paper. Using a magic marker, draw five lines horizontally across each piece of paper to make six equal sections. Laminate the papers.

Cut the laminated, lined paper in half vertically so you have six cards measuring 4 1/2" x 6". Take the highlighter tape and cut it into strips. Place the strips of highlighter tape on the six spaces on each card.

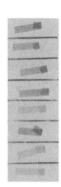

Be sure to make a "grab tab" on each strip of tape. Turn one edge of each piece over so that the end is not sticky. This is where students will grab the tape to put it on and take it off when finished. Each student will have his/her own strip of paper with tape.

Reading Box Contents

When boxes are initially created, they are filled with familiar, old favorite reading materials.

> # Familiarity with books allows students to be independent and easily apply, practice, and utilize reading strategies

We want our students reading. That is the ultimate goal. We want our students to attend to the print and pictures. If students do not like books, and they are "flippers" just flipping through the pages and saying "I'm done," then we need to turn them on to the print and pictures. The reading box is full of many items that are not books. Books are the ultimate goal, but for some children, just getting them to read a cereal box or the name of a friend is a monumental step. The reading boxes are full of items to read.

The following items have been used very successfully in reading boxes.

Class Lists
Students are so excited to read each others' names. Make a list of names of students in your class. For young children, put pictures of classmates next to their names to help with the reading. Students often pair up and one person reads the first name while the other reads the last name.

School Lists
The class lists were so successful that we created school lists in the reading boxes. School lists are names of any persons that are associated with the school. Your list may include: principal, secretary, teachers, custodians, cooks, crossing guards, bus drivers, etc. Put pictures next to the names for younger children.

Box Books
Box books are great ways to use environmental print. Have students bring in cereal or similar boxes. Cut the tops and bottoms off the boxes. The boxes will now fold down flat. Put 3-5 boxes together, punch two holes, and tie together with yarn or use chicken rings to put them together into a box book.

There are so many things that can be done with the boxes in addition to using them as books of environmental print. Before you cut and tie the boxes together, use them for graphing activities. For example, have students bring in breakfast food boxes. Graph them according to the ones you eat hot or cold, ones you eat with a fork, spoon, or by hand, etc. The same can be done with animal boxes: dog bones, guinea pig food, parrot food, peanuts, cat food, etc. Simple greeting cards can also be used.

Book Covers

Many hard covered books have a book jacket on them. Take the jackets off the books and put three or four book covers together, punch holes, and tie them together. These can be used in similar fashion as the box books. Your librarian can be a great resource for this activity.

Wordless Books

The students' language development increases as they tell stories about the wordless books. Storytelling helps students organize and sequence a story orally. They work with the concepts of beginning, middle, and end, as well as story elements. These books help students attend to pictures.

Books

Two requirements need to be met by books before they can be placed in reading boxes. First, they need to be familiar to the students. Students must have worked with or heard the story at least one time. Second, the books need to be at students' independent reading levels. The little readers that go along with basal series are great to use.

Poems

Seasonal poems are fun for students to read over and over again. I found that poetry books were a bit overwhelming for some students. Take the books apart and put in only a couple of poems at a time. You could also type or write the poems out on paper and place the papers in the reading boxes. (See Appendix for recommended poetry books).

Magazines

Weekly Reader, Scholastic News, or any other weekly/monthly newsletter that you use in your classroom can be placed in the reading boxes. Sometimes these reading materials are only looked at and discussed one time by the whole class. Utilizing them again for the reading boxes gets some repeated reading of content area materials for students.

Pledge of Allegiance

Listen to your students recite the pledge. Many of them really do not know what the words are. Make copies of the Pledge of Allegiance and add them to reading boxes.

Science and Social Studies Connections

Take some important paragraphs from your science and social studies curriculum. Type or write so the print is large for students as expository text can be more difficult for them to read and understand than narrative texts.

Comics

These are short, quick reads for students.

Charts and Chants From Around Your Room

Anything that is displayed in your room can be copied or typed and put in the box. I found that my students often read the things on the wall only when I took them over to them and we did some choral and shared reading. Now they are reading those things many times on their own. I have seen a lot of improvement in my whole class reading of chants and charts because students are practicing them more!

If you have class rules posted, put copies of them in the reading boxes. Look around your room at all the things you hang up for students to read. Any of those items may be used.

Menus

There are two kinds of menus that can be used: school menus and restaurant menus. On Fridays when menus are passed out at school for the following week, they are also put into the reading boxes. Many restaurants have donated their menus for students to use.

Bag Books

Paper bags are great ways to use environmental print. Have students bring in bags from different stores and restaurants. Put 3-5 bags together, punch holes and tie them together with yarn to make a "bag book."

Brochures

Brochures can be found at hotels, restaurants, travel agencies, parks, etc. They are excellent samples of expository texts for students.

Notices

Any notice that is sent home, if appropriate, can be placed into the boxes.

Spelling Words

Each week put in your spelling list. Leave them in the boxes all year. It is a great review for students throughout the school year to see words they had from months before.

Coordination with all Specialists:

Art: Some art teachers have created an "Artist of the Month" bulletin board. Each month a different artist's picture, biography, and art work are displayed. Use the information from this display to write a class "report" for the reading boxes. Below are examples from a first grade and a fourth grade.

Claude Monet was a famous artist born over 100 years ago in France. He always loved to paint landscapes and seascapes. He liked to show how scenes look different at certain times of the day because of light. This kind of painting is called Impressionism.

He painted many pictures of water and nature. He painted more than 2,000 paintings that sell for millions of dollars. He died at 86 years of age.

Claude Monet was a famous artist. He was born in 1840 in Paris, France. He loved painting from an early age. His friends nicknamed him "Dandy" because even though he was broke, he wore expensive shirts with ruffled cuffs.

Monet painted many seascapes and landscapes of the French countryside. He painted a picture of a sunrise and called it Impressions: Sunrise. From this painting's title came the term "Impressionism." Impressionists liked to show how different types of natural light affected objects in their painting. This kind of painting was one of the most unique art movements in history.

He painted more than 2,000 paintings that now sell for millions of dollars. He died in 1926 at 86 years of age.

Music: Songs are great resources. Also, whatever else is being taught in music can be written and put into the boxes.

Physical Education: Directions to games or a list of vocabulary words can be used.

Library: Use information about the card catalog, authors, books, etc. Before students leave the library, write down a list of facts they learned. Put them in the box.

Computer: Write out and put in directions for using the computer. Use pictures and vocabulary of different computer parts: keyboard, disc, disc drive, and monitor.

Baseball Cards
Any kind of sport's card: baseball, football, and basketball are great to use.

Calendar Area
Think about your calendar area. There is a wealth of reading going on there: days of the week, months of the year, holidays, birthdays, seasons.

Color Words
Depending upon the grade level, use color words other than the traditional primary colors: teal, chartreuse, etc.

Vocabulary Words from Science and Social Studies Units

Sight Words / Dolch Lists / Fry List

Word Wall Words

Guided Reading Group Materials
Materials in the reading box can be directly coordinated with your guided reading groups. Anything you talk about and teach in the guided reading groups can be put into the reading boxes. Anything I would write on the whiteboard during the lesson is now also written on index cards and/or pieces of paper. Those papers and index cards go right into the reading box. Instead of erasing on the whiteboard, which for some students means out of sight, out of mind, information gets written on something that students can refer to over and over again.

Teacher is working with a guided reading group. Four students are in the background group working with reading boxes.

Management of the Background Groups when Using Reading Boxes

When you call the groups, B and C for example, group B (guided reading group) comes to the reading table, while group C (background group) goes to its work place, which is either on the floor or at a table to the left or right of you. If students are meeting on the floor, they sit on the colored circles.

Reader of the Day

The Reader of the Day is the student who gets the reading box. While his/her peers are taking their places, he/she is the only one who touches the box. This has alleviated many disagreements within the group about who is in charge of getting the box.

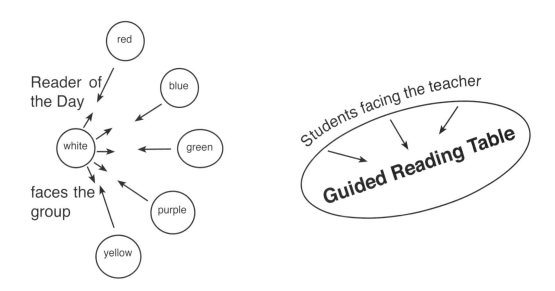

Students in the group face the Reader of the Day.

The Reader of the Day begins by choosing anything in the box and reads it aloud to the group. This helps the background group start calmly and as a team. It also allows for one child to read orally to an audience. The Reader of the Day may do any of the following read-aloud activities:

Traditional Read-Aloud
The child reads the material just like the teacher would during a typical read-aloud session. He/she reads and then shows the picture. Any material in the reading box can be done as a traditional read-aloud.

Retelling of the Story
This procedure can be done with only two items: wordless books or books with print. If the Reader of the Day chooses a wordless book, then he/she tells a story as the pictures are shown. The Reader of the Day could also retell any book in the box. The student must tell the group that he/she is retelling the story, not actually reading the book. Often students who are not confident readers choose this method.

Choral Reading with the Whole Group
The Reader of the Day picks any reading material from the box and the group reads it chorally.

Popcorn Reading
The Reader of the Day reads a page aloud, and then asks a group member to reread that page aloud. The reading task goes back and forth between the leader and group members.

The Reader of the Day may decide to do this same procedure in the opposite order. He/she shows a page to a group member who will read it aloud, and then the Reader of the Day repeats that page orally. When the read-aloud is over, students will read silently. The Reader of the Day takes the colored circle cards (see page 30), mixes them up and puts them face-down on the floor. He/she then picks up one card at a time. The child sitting on that chosen color picks his/her reading material first. This routine is continued until all of the students have one item to read.

The Reader of the Day is the last one to choose a reading item from the box. This procedure has stopped the problem of students all pushing and rushing to get into the box first. As students finish reading, they put back their item and choose another on their own. Usually students do not all finish reading at the same time, so each is in the reading box at different times.

Partner Reading

Children have asked if they can partner up and read together in the background group. Here are some ways for students to read the texts together.

Chorally
Partners read the text together.

Read, Retell, Read, Retell
One child reads a page and then the partner retells in his own words what happened on that page. This helps with listening skills, retelling and comprehension. Students change roles after each page.

Read, Repeat, Read, Repeat
One child reads a page and then the partner rereads the same page. This helps with fluency and comprehension. Students change roles after each page.

Pass the Reading
One child begins reading and then passes the reading to his partner. The reading gets passed anywhere on the page. It cannot be passed at the bottom of the page. This requires the partner to follow along while the other is reading so each knows where to begin when the reading is passed. They "pass the reading" by either saying their partner's name or passing an object to their partner. Some things they have passed are a stuffed animal, a ball, or a chip.

Readers' Theatre
Students choose parts and read the story as a readers' theatre. They should not say the word "said." This helps students read with expression and attentiveness to punctuation.

Read and Question
One student reads and his partner asks a question about what was just read.

Changing Materials in the Reading Boxes

Materials should be changed when the guided reading groups change, every 4-6 weeks. On the last Thursday or Friday when guided reading groups are going to meet, students work together to clean out and change materials in their reading boxes. All of the materials in the reading boxes are taken out. This is a great time to conduct some fluency assessments. Students each choose something to read orally to the group. Everyone reads something until all of the items that were in the box have been read. You are expecting fluent reading of these texts as students have been working with them for several weeks. Students can each put back a favorite reading item. Now, as new books, poems, songs, etc. are worked with, they are added to the reading boxes. There should be about a 3 to 1 ratio of materials to students.

Making the Reading Box Manipulative

The following activities are for emergent level readers who may need some hands-on activities to help them focus and attend to the reading materials.

On one side of the box are three laminated index cards (see page 28). These cards have certain things written on them for students to look for as they read. Using the highlighter tape, students find certain things related to pictures and/or print and mark them. These are optional activities for students to do.

These cards get changed either weekly or every other week.

Index Card #1 - Options

characters

Write the word "characters" on the index card.

Using picture books with one line of text or less
Students find the characters on each page and mark them with the tape. One of the first prompts used with beginning emergent readers is to look at the pictures. This activity helps students to really attend to and study the pictures.

Using books that have pictures as well as four or more lines of text per page
Students look for illustrations of characters and mark them on each page. Students also mark any text that tells about the character(s). This leads students into making some inferences. For example, the book may not say the character is shy but it can be inferred by the character's actions or how he/she behaves.

> **setting**

Write the word "setting" on the index card.

Using picture books with one line of text or less
Students look for the setting on each page and mark it with the tape. This again helps students to really attend to and study the pictures.

Using books that have pictures as well as four or more lines of text per page
Students look for the setting on each page and mark it. Students also mark any text that tells about the setting.

> **title**

Write the word "title" on the index card.

Using picture books with one line of text or less
Students look for illustrations that back up and support why the book may have its title. They mark the pictures with the tape. This gives students practice in previewing the title of a book and making predictions about the story.

Using books that have pictures as well as four or more lines of text per page
Students look for illustrations and text that back up and support why the book may have its title. They mark the pictures and text with the tape. This gives students practice in previewing the title of a book and making predictions about the story. It also helps students with comprehension of the story.

> **red**

Put a color word on the index card. Students mark everything in the pictures that is that color.

Index Card #2 - Options

Using the preceding strategy of finding and marking, the following suggestions can be put on the second index card.

Sight words
Letters
Words
Contractions
Verbs with "ing" ending
Verbs with "ed" ending
Plurals
Homophones
Synonyms
Antonyms
Words for "said"

Anything being taught or reviewed can be put on the card.

Index Card #3 - Options

Using the preceding strategy of finding and marking, the following suggestions can be put on the third index card.

Anything that corresponds to your phonics and spelling curriculum. For example:
"ay" words
"ai" words
    short "a" words
"er" or "ir" words

More assessment of the background group doing these activities is discussed on page 55.

It is too difficult to check every single page, in every book, for every child, to see what has been marked. Have students tell each other what they marked and why before they take the tape off the text. This helps students be accountable for their markings.

LITERATURE DISCUSSION BOXES

Quick Overview of Literature Discussion Boxes

What are discussion boxes?

Literature discussion boxes are boxes or plastic tubs of reading materials created especially for each guided reading group to use when it is meeting as a background group. These differ from reading boxes because only one title with multiple copies is available as all students will be working with the same book.

How are discussion boxes organized?

The reading material in the box is leveled to be as perfect a match as possible for that group of students. Dictionaries and thesauruses are in the boxes.

Who leads the group's discussions?

Each student will be responsible to lead a specific discussion about something in the book.

When are discussion boxes used?

Discussion boxes are used while the teacher is working with a guided reading group.

Where are discussion boxes used?

Discussion boxes are used on the floor directly to the right or left of the teacher and his/her guided reading group.

Why are discussion boxes created and used?

Discussion boxes are used with fluent readers to talk about a book in depth. Students come to the group to share and gain insights from each other.

Literature Discussion Box Contents

Put an index card or piece of paper on one side of each discussion box. Write the names of students in the group that will using that particular box in the background group.

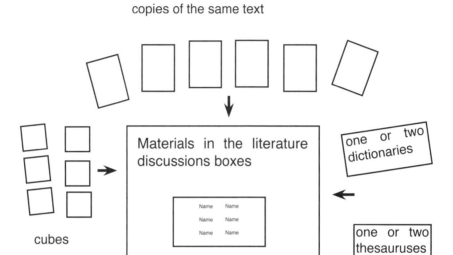

copies of the same text

Materials in the literature discussions boxes

Name	Name
Name	Name
Name	Name

cubes

one or two dictionaries

one or two thesauruses

Cubes

The following pages will show you how to make and set-up discussion cubes. This section shows how to get them ready. Explanations of the cubes begin on page 48. Using the reproducible found in the Appendix, make copies of the cube out of oaktag in different colors.

Cube #1

This is a vocabulary cube. Label the sides of the first cube with the following:

Synonym

Antonym

Definition

Sentence

Connect to you

Importance to the story

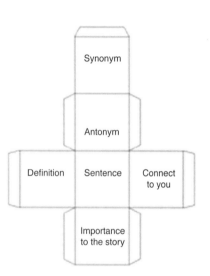

Cube #2

This is a questions word cube. Label the sides of the second cube with the following:

Who

What

Where

Why

When

How

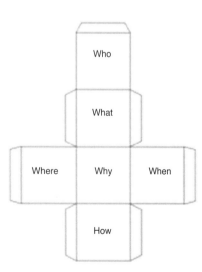

Cube #3

This is a character cube. Label the sides of the third cube with the following:

Personality

Physical appearance

Your opinion about the character: Why?

How are you alike?

How are you different?

What has happened to the character in your reading assignment?

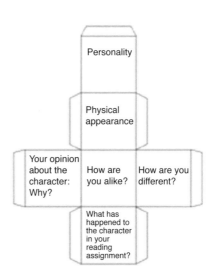

Cubes #4

This is an "I wonder" cube. Label the sides of the fourth cube with the following:

I wonder who...

I wonder what...

I wonder where...

I wonder why...

I wonder when...

I wonder how...

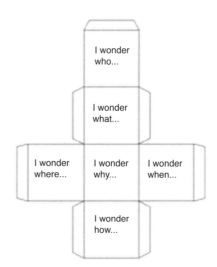

Cube #5

This is a story element cube. Label the sides of the fifth cube with the following:

Characters

Setting

Problem / Solution

Plot

Theme

Predict or Create

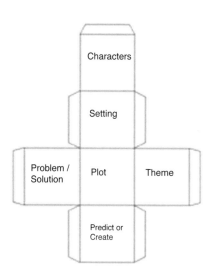

Cubes #6

This is a compare and contrast cube. Label the sides of the sixth cube with the following:

Point of View

Setting

Problem / Solution

You and _____

Characters

Your opinion and that of a character

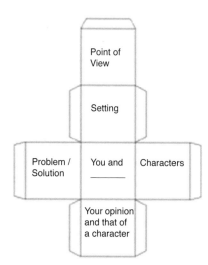

Cube #7

This is a connection cube. Label the sides of the seventh cube with the following:

Text-to-Self

Text-to-Self

Text-to-Text

Text-to-Text

Text-to-World

Text-to-World

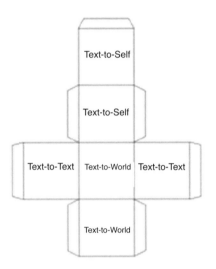

Cubes #8

This is a read-aloud cube. Label the sides of the eighth cube with the following:

Emotional

Descriptive

Ah-ha Moment

Leave it out

Leave it in

Clues about the future

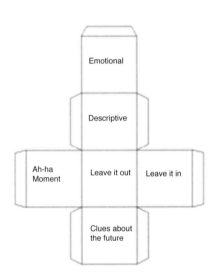

The book *Cubes: Discussion Activities for Literacy and Skill Development* is a great resource to use for making cubes.

Management of the Background Groups when Using Literature Discussion Boxes

Students using discussion boxes are all reading the same text, story, or novel. There is no reading assignment in the background group. Students have already read the text. They come to the group ready to discuss, share perceptions, and converse about their reading assignment. You want to create an open-ended dialogue between students in which they extend their learning and move from literal, descriptive talk to a deeper understanding of their reading.

What text is being used and when does the reading get done?
These two questions are continually asked in reference to the literature discussion boxes being used in the background group:

What text is being used in the background group?
When is the reading getting done?

Below are four options to answer these two questions. The first two suggestions are for groups who need repetition and support. The last two options are for more independent readers.

Option 1
Students use the same text that was used during a whole group lesson/activity. It could be the story from the basal/anthology, a section in the science or social studies book, a weekly reader, poem, article, etc. There is no new reading involved for students before the background group meets, as the selection has already been read and discussed in whole group. Students will revisit the selection again and rediscuss, reread, and review.

Option 2
This is identical to option one except the selection used is the same as was used in the guided reading group.

Notice in options one and two that no new reading is involved. Students will reread, scan and skim for information, and have conversations about previously read and discussed texts. These are great options for students who were a part of a whole group lesson with a basal text or content area text, but really need a second dose of the text to increase their comprehension.

Options three and four have reading assignments that students must complete before they meet. These are for students who are more independent readers. They comprehend well and do not need as much scaffolding in vocabulary and comprehension as the students working with options one and two.

Option 3
Students will use the same text that is being used in guided reading. When the guided reading group is finished, students will be given a new assignment that must be read before they meet as a background group the next day. Silently reading the text can be done for homework, during SSR time, and/or during seatwork/assignment time.

Option 4
Students are reading a second book specifically for background group time. Students together assign themselves what to read and sometimes assign a focus for their next discussion time. This option is for your very fluent, independent readers.

Notice these four options go from a lot of scaffolding on the teacher's part to little or no direction from the teacher.

Using the Discussion Cubes

On the following pages are ideas and suggestions about the cubes students could be utilizing in the background group, and how to manage and organize discussions. Each cube is really a topic that helps run the discussion and also helps students manage the group.

The cubes are always rolled clockwise, so there is no arguing about whose turn it is. Students always know when it will be their turn to roll the cube and talk. The rule is: the one with the cube does the talking! If students want to respond to each other, they must raise their hands and have the cube thrown to them. This has helped students to not all talk at once and really listen to each other.

Every child will roll every cube in a clockwise manner. Now there is also no arguing about what cube each student has because everyone is going to roll every cube. One cube is not harder or easier to be in charge of than another. And if there is a favorite cube, it doesn't matter who is in charge of it because everyone will get a turn to roll that cube. You can assign students a certain cube that they would be in charge of, or students can choose themselves.

When the group first meets, a decision about which cube to start with is made, either by students or the teacher. The only cube that stays out is the one that is being used to start the discussion. All other cubes are placed behind students, back in the discussion box, or out of the way somewhere.

The leader, the one whose cube is being used, rolls the cube first and applies whatever was rolled to the text being used. The leader then throws the cube to the next person in a clockwise manner. That student rolls the cube and applies whatever was rolled to the text being used. That student then throws the cube back to the leader who in turn throws it to the next child in a clockwise manner. The cube always comes back to the leader who will throw it to the child whose turn is next. This continues until all of the students have rolled the cube.

The cubes help to manage taking turns, making sure that everyone gets a turn to share and is an attentive audience participant. Remember the rule is:
> *the one with the cube does the talking and everyone else listens.*

The cubes also direct the conversation so that students have a springboard that leads to critical and thought-provoking discussions.

Child #1, the leader for this cube, begins by rolling her cube on the floor. She discusses what was rolled. She then throws the cube to child #2, who rolls it on the floor. He discusses what was rolled and then gives the cube back to the leader.

Child #1 throws the cube to child #3, who rolls it on the floor. He discusses what was rolled and then gives the cube back to the leader.

Child #1 throws the cube to child #4, who rolls it on the floor. He discusses what was rolled and then gives the cube back to the leader.

Now all four students have had a turn to roll and discuss this cube. If there is time left for more discussion, the group continues in a clockwise position. Child #2 takes out his cube and the above process is done with the second cube. If more time is still left after the second cube is discussed, child #3 takes out his cube and the above process is done with the third cube.

Vocabulary Cube

If using options three or four from page 48, each student brings a vocabulary word or words from the text to share. If using options one or two from page 47, then vocabulary words are already written on index cards from the whole group discussion and are in the box. The student who rolls first either shares his/her chosen word or picks a card from the box. He/she tells what the word is and on which page the word is found. (The page number is written on the card or told by the student choosing that particular word.) All students open their books to that page and find the word. The student in charge reads three sentences: the sentence where the word was found, as well as the sentence before and the sentence after. Now he/she rolls the cube and applies the word to whatever side is face-up.

Synonym

> The student gives a synonym for the vocabulary word. A thesaurus, which is in the box, may be used.

Antonym

> The student tells an antonym for the vocabulary word.

Definition

> The student gives a definition of the vocabulary word. The student gives the meaning in his/her own words. A dictionary, which is in the box, may be used.

Sentence

> The word is used in a sentence by the student. The sentence must be about home, school, or the student. This stops students repeating the sentence from the book.

Connect to you

> The student tells how the word is connected to his/her life. For example, if the word is "blustery," a connection might be: "I do not like blustery days because I don't like to be cold."

Importance to the story

> The student discusses why that word is important to the story and why that particular word might have been used instead of another word. Students talk about the subtleties of the word that was used. For example: "blustery" instead of "cold."

Question Word Cube

This cube can be used in one of two ways. The student who rolls the cube can ask a question based on the question word that was rolled. For example, if "what" is rolled, then the student would have to ask a "what" question and would call on a group member to answer. Or the student who rolled the question word would be asked that kind of question from someone in the group.

Students have high-level, open-ended prompts available to use for this cube. Without the prompts, I found students tended to ask literal questions and most required only a one-word answer. With the question prompts, their questions are fabulous, high-level, and thought-provoking. Some examples of prompts are:

How would the story be different if _____ were not in the story?
What do you think_____ will do next? Why?
Why do think _____ did _____?
Where does the character get inner strength?
Who would the character's best friend be in this classroom? Why?

The book *Question Prompts: Taking Comprehension to a Higher Level* is a great resource to use for open-ended prompts.

Character Cube

You want students to learn how characters' personalities are revealed through the things they say, the things they do, the way they think, how they react to situations, etc. This cube also helps with scanning and skimming for information, as well as using textual support, because students are required to go back into the book to confirm and support all of their answers. For example, if "physical appearance" is rolled and a child states the character had brown hair, is ten years old and wears sneakers, then all group members would have to go into the book to find these statements and prove them. Although the question and answer are not high-level and thought-provoking, students are working on the process of scanning and skimming for information.

Story Element Cube

These discussions are based on the story element that is rolled. If a student rolls "setting," he/she must talk about the setting. Following are examples of setting discussions.

    Describe the setting.
    Why is the setting important to the story?
    How would the story be different if the setting was different?
    What is your opinion of the setting? Would you like to live there? Why or why not?

The side that says "Predict or Create" can be used a number of different ways. If using a book or story that has not been completed, students can predict what they think will happen next. If using a text that has been completed, students can create a new chapter, a different ending, a sequel, a prequel, or tell where the character might be ten years from now. Students do not write but have conversations. This is the students' favorite side of the cube. I have heard some very lively conversation and ideas with this side of the story element cube.

Compare and Contrast Cube

This is a skill that students work with a lot in reading and writing. Putting it as a part of their discussion groups has helped them become more detailed in their writing and more thorough in their reading. Below are ideas for each side of the compare/contrast cube.

Characters: Students choose two characters from the book to compare and contrast.

Setting: Students compare and contrast the setting of the book to where they live. They could also compare and contrast what is happening in their story now versus if the setting was different.

Problem/Solution: Students compare and contrast how they would have handled problems and solutions in the story versus the way the characters handled them. They could compare and contrast different ways to handle problems in the book and what different solutions there might be.

You and _____: Students choose a character from the book to compare and contrast with themselves.

Point of View: Compare and contrast the story from different points of view of the characters.

Another Opinion: Students choose a character's opinion about something and compare and contrast it with another character's opinion. Students could also compare and contrast their own opinion about something versus the character's opinion.

Connection Cube:

Students' discussions are based on what kind of connection is rolled. When Text-to-Self is rolled, students talk about how the text can be related to themselves. When Text-to-Text is rolled, students discuss what other texts the current one reminds them of and why. When Text-to-World is rolled, students converse about the theme and messages the author has for his/her writing.

Read-Aloud Cube

This cube gives students practice in reading to an audience, as well as increasing their fluency. It also helps them read for deeper messages and meaning. Students choose a part of the text to read aloud based on what is rolled. They must explain their reasons for choosing the specific text.

Emotional: Students choose a part that is emotional. It makes them smile, laugh, cry, get annoyed, get frustrated, etc.

Descriptive: Students choose a part that is very descriptive. It may contain similes, metaphors, descriptive language, etc.

Ah-ha Moment: Students choose a part where the character or the reader had an ah-ha moment. Something all of a sudden becomes clear or something is finally understood.

Leave it out: Students choose a passage they feel could have been left out. The passage has no impact to what happens. It is a boring part. It is a part that gives trivial information that really isn't important to the story.

Leave it in: Students pick a passage they feel is very important to the story. If the passage was to be left out, a deeper understanding of something might be missed. This could also be the main idea of the reading assignment.

Clues about the future: Students choose a part or parts that give them clues as to what might happen in the future.

Modeling is one of the most important components of a student's success, enjoyment, and independence with the cubes. Model the cubes whole class with a read-aloud. If you work with two cubes a week, in four weeks your students will be ready to utilize them in a background group. My biggest mistake was to not model enough. I thought, how hard is this? You throw the cube, discuss what was rolled, and move on to the next person. But obviously, it is much more complicated than that! If we want high-level application and utilization with these discussion cubes, then they must be modeled in a deliberate, detailed way with multiple opportunities for applying them to reading.

Assessment of Background Groups

When your guided reading instruction is complete, give them a three to four minute activity to do independently. If they are tired and unable to focus anymore, give them some clay to make letters, words, and/or things from the book they have just read. If they are able to attend a bit more, either pair students up and have them reread the book(s) you have been working with, or give them a new reading assignment. You are now free to visit the background group.

You can assess students in the background group daily using an anecdotal record notebook. This is a three-ring notebook that has lined paper in it. Put pieces of masking tape on pages to make a section for each of your students. Write their names on the pieces of tape.

If the background group is working with a reading box, you can sit by a child and ask him/her things such as:

What is this sight word?
Can you find the word "said" on this page?
I will read this page and you point to the words while I read.
Please read this page to me.
Where is the letter "M?"
Tell me what is happening in the picture.
Read an item from the box to me.
Etc.

This list is endless! Look at all the information you can get in a very short period of time; literally, in a couple of minutes. Write the information in your notebook and move on to the second child. You can usually assess two students every day.

If the background group is working with a discussion box, then you can sit with the whole group and ask some key questions to determine whether or not they comprehend the main idea and most important details in that reading assignment. You can also check on knowledge of vocabulary words or anything that may be confusing to them.

OVERVIEW OF PART 1

	First	Next	Then	Last
Teacher	Calls two reading groups.	Works with the "front" group in a guided reading lesson.	After 20 minutes gives the guided reading group some clay or a reading assignment to be done at the table.	Assesses individual students or the whole background group.
Front Group	Meets at the guided reading table when called by the teacher.	Works with teacher in a guided reading format.	After 20 minutes make letters, words, or things from the book out of clay. May read with a partner. May read independently.	All clean up and begin independent work.
Background Group: Reading Boxes	Meets on the floor in close proximity to the teacher.	Reader of the Day gets the reading box and begins with a read-aloud.	After the read-aloud, students get their own materials and read silently.	Students are assessed by teacher. All clean up and begin independent work.
Background Group: Literature Discussion Boxes	Meets on the floor in close proximity to the teacher.	Each student is in charge of a certain discussion. Cubes are used as a management tool.	Continue discussions.	Groups are assessed by teacher. All clean up and begin independent work.

Part 2

What Are the Other Students Doing While I Am with a Guided Reading Group?

WHAT ARE THE OTHER STUDENTS DOING WHILE I AM WITH A GUIDED READING GROUP?

This question can make or break any kind of grouping situation. Students need to be actively engaged in meaningful assignments at their ability levels. If assignments are too hard, you have the "I don't get it" line that forms at your guided reading table. If assignments are too easy, you hear, "I'm done. Now what do I do?"

There are two kinds of assignments to think about. The first kind of assignment is the work students do at their seats with workbooks, worksheets, new skills, etc. They are often whole class assignments where everyone gets the same work to complete. They usually include new directions that change per page or on a daily basis.

When working with these kinds of assignments, the teacher needs to be accessible for questions. These assignments are often not multi-leveled, so they will be too hard for some and too easy for others. You need to be available to help those who need support and challenge those who need enrichment.

The second kind of assignments are those given to students while the teacher is with a guided reading group and not available for help. These assignments need to be multi-leveled so that different ability levels can successfully complete the tasks. They need to be tasks that can be applied to any book, any skill, and any level.

The tasks and directions need to be consistent. The directions never change. "How do I complete the assignment?" "Where are the materials?" "What do I do?" The answers to these questions never change. Students will know how and what to do with the assignments if they are consistent all year. What changes each week is how the students apply and utilize learned skills with these assignments. Part 2 focuses on these types of assignments.

Building Foundations

Foundations support everything that is built upon them.

A lighthouse cannot lead and guide if it does not have a solid foundation which cannot be seen.

In a classroom, part of the foundation is students knowing how to work independently while the teacher is with a group. They need to know how to complete the assignment, as well as what to do when they get stuck or when they complete their work.

Modeling

One of the biggest mistakes in the classroom has been not building a strong enough foundation. Teachers show students how to do something once and then expect them to complete the assignment correctly. This usually does not happen.

Modeling plays an integral part in how successfully and easily students are able to complete assignments. Any assignment students are asked to complete while the teacher is with a group must be significantly modeled a number of times in a number of different ways.

Think of a ladder.

Your goal is to get students to the top rung of the ladder.

The old paradigm might look like the ladder to the right.

There is too much distance for students to reach from the bottom rung all the way to the top rung. They will probably fall.

In the classroom, the "falling" may be these:

students interrupting the guided reading group,

students just sitting and not getting the work done,

students walking around the room,

behavior problems.

You need to give students support so they can and will make it to the top rung. The modeling now looks like this:

Independent: student successfully work alone!
Students are given the assignment to complete independently.

Partner: students work with a partner.
Students are given the assignment and they work with partners to complete it.

Small Group: students work in groups.
Students are given the assignment and they work in a small group to complete it.

Whole Group: students work with the teacher.
The teacher still does all the writing but most of the answers and ideas come from students. Students have taken control of the assignment and activity, but the teacher is the scribe. Also, work through problems that may occur as students are working: What do you do if you get stuck? Where do you go for help? What do you do if you think you're done?

Whole Group: students watch.
The teacher does everything. Students just watch. Students may ask questions or you may ask them questions, but they do no writing. All they do is watch.

During guided reading instruction you want the least amount of interruptions possible, so any assignment given during this time should be modeled in the above way.

As you use this ladder as a basis for your modeling, keep in mind you may skip one rung if you feel students are grasping quickly, but never skip more than one rung.

Remember that the assignments being modeled are assignments that students will be using all year, so the foundation you are building will support your classroom management for the year.

ASSIGNMENT CATEGORIES

This section presents a wealth of assignments that can be given to students while guided reading groups are in session. These assignments are organized into five different categories. Duke the Dog will introduce each category. On the top of each activity page will be an icon of Duke. The icon will tell you which category is being addressed while students are working through the specific assignment.

Writing Activities

Students are often given assignments, such as writing stories, describing characters, telling about the books they've read, etc. These tasks require students to "put it all together" and create an organized piece of writing. Students need lots of practice with simple, short tasks before moving onto more connected pieces of writing. The more students practice labeling, writing lists, describing items, etc., the easier the longer pieces of writing become. The more students write, the better writers they become.

Some of the assignments in this category are short, easy tasks that get children generating words and beginning to put something down on paper. Other tasks are more detailed and require more from students. Most of the activities are multi-leveled so that students of different abilities can successfully complete them. For some activities, there will be assignments for beginning writers as well as for fluent writers.

Literature Connections

These assignments can be used with any story or book students are using. They can be stories from your guided reading groups, a whole group read aloud, or from your basal/anthology.

Language Arts

The suggestions here will be general ideas. Use these ideas to reinforce and practice your specific content for the week or to review concepts already taught. Your curriculum will dictate specific assignments. Phonics, spelling, and listening skills are some of the topics covered in this category.

Sight Vocabulary

These high frequency words do not follow the typical phonetic rules. They do not represent spelling patterns. One of the keys to sight vocabulary acquisition is multiple exposures. Many of these assignments have students finding, making, reading, and writing the words over and over again. Activities in this category will reinforce the reading and writing of sight vocabulary.

Additional Activities

These activities include reading, writing, content areas, and art.

WRITING ACTIVITIES

Top Ten

Make a chart like some of the examples below. Notice all of the charts have two things in common:

A title that says: Top Ten _____.

Things to do with the Top Ten list should a student complete his/her list before the allotted time.

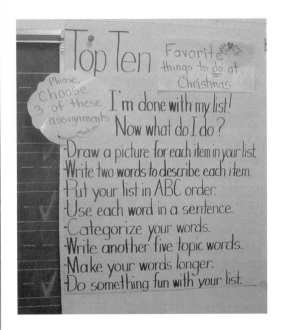

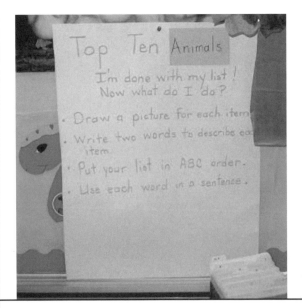

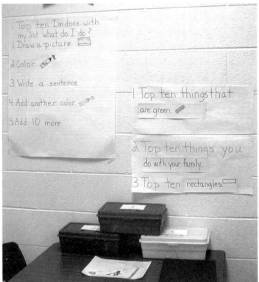

Notice the materials and scaffolding at this Top Ten center.

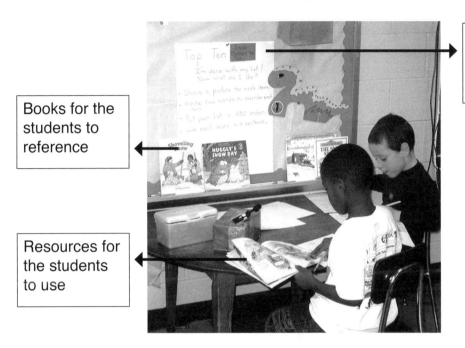

Top Ten
Winter Items

Books for the
students to
reference

Resources for
the students
to use

Each week the only change to this center is the topic for the list. If you laminate this chart, then all you need to do each week is wipe off the old topic and write in the new topic. If your chart is not laminated, then just change the topic by taping a piece of paper with the new topic on the chart. When students have completed their lists, they may choose any of the extensions listed on the chart. I used to have a fill-in form for students to use with this activity, but found that just lined or unlined paper can be used. It saves you time from having to copy the form and putting it at the center. It also requires that students take more ownership in choosing paper and setting it up.

You can tie this activity to any of your curriculum areas:

Science
things that are living
things that are non-living
kinds of weather
transportation
things on a farm
things that float
things that a magnet attracts
things that are sweet, sour, salty, etc.

Math
things that are round, square, etc.
things that are longer than a foot (12")
things that are shorter than a foot (12")
ways to make the number 3,4,17, 58, etc.
      (addition /subtraction facts)
ways to make $1.25
things that come in 6's or 12's (half-dozen or dozen)
odd numbers
even numbers

Language Arts
words to describe a character
words to describe a setting
verbs
adjectives
two-syllable words
compound words
words instead of "said"
words instead of "nice"
pairs of synonyms (cellar/basement)
pairs of antonyms (happy/sad)

Tie in your spelling and phonics each week. Students write ten words that have the pattern, sound, rule, etc., that have been studied during the week.

Social Studies
things you find at the beach
differences between city and country
community helpers
things you see in the spring, summer, fall, winter
things in a post office
ocean words
ways to travel
things found on a map

Top 10 Winter Items

scarf
hat
boot
jacket
truck
sled
pants
bucket
shovel

glove
(on back side of paper}

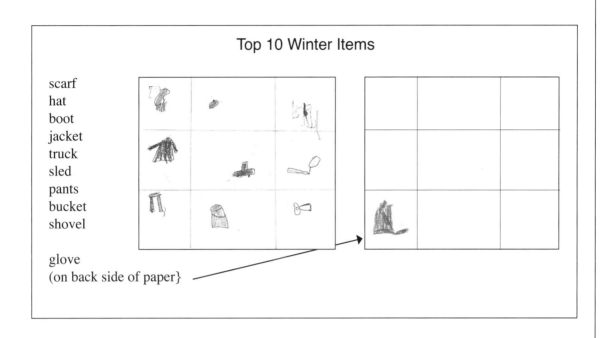

Top 10 Friends

Top Ten
Pilgrims

1 corn
2. Bread
3. Mayflower
4. gold
5 church
6. corn plants
7. clothes X heavy
8. nats old
9. fort small
10. Virginia big

corn	bread	mayflower	gold
yellow	food	boat	slickerish
yummy	good	old	shiny
vegetable	healthy	watery	pretty
long	brownish	big	rich
plant	long	long	treasure
church	**crop**	**clothes**	**nats**
worship	plant	old	dusty
big	huge	brownish	tall
bells	fields	long sleeves	big
god	good	big	brown
sunday	tasty	hottish	round

fort	Virginia
old	state
small	big
house	old
tall	long

ABC order
1 bread
2 church
3 clothes
4 corn
5 crops

Top ten
Careers

1. fireman

2. police

3. Teacher

4. life guard

5. mail man

6. doctor

7. chef

8. goverment

9. mayor

10. president

Top ten For things we learned in the viedo we watched

1 bees dance to communicate

2. bees take nectar and turn it into honey

3 bees have to take honey before winter

4 bees work together

5 bees share food

6 bees use honey to feed the laravas

7 bees have a specail smell

8 if you are not a bee the bees will sting you

9 bees live in a hive

10 bears destroy bee hives

Top Ten Things
You Would Find In a
Garden

1. plants
2. flowers
3. tomatoes
4. sugar snap pees
5. seeds
6. rose bushes
7. trees
8. soil
9. corn
10. carrots

Top ten
ecosystems

1. Tundra
2. Grasslands
3. desert
4. rainforest
5. oceans
6. wetlands
7. pond
8. lake
9. forest
10. river
11. fields
12. sea
13. sky

Picture Tales

Fill a box or container with all kinds of pictures: magazine pictures, calendar pictures, greeting cards, post cards, and photos. Students choose a picture, glue it onto a piece of paper, and make it into part of a bigger scene.

There are two different writing assignments students can work on with these pictures. They can write descriptions about their pictures or they can write stories about their pictures. There really is no change to this center on a weekly basis. It is a continuous writing center. When students have finished an assignment, they take another picture and start again. The only change you may have is adding pictures that tie to your science and social studies units or seasonal pictures.

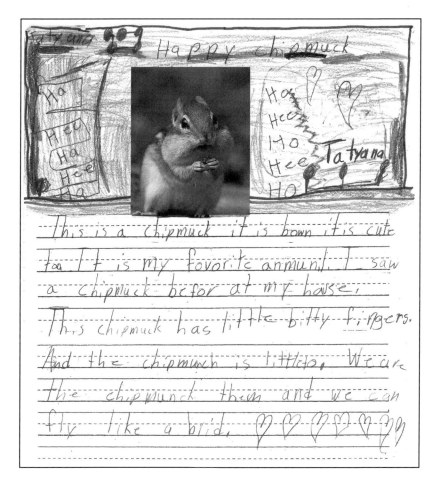

Happy chipmuck

Ha
Hee
Ha
Hee
Ha

Ha
Hee
Ho
Hee   Tatyana
Ho

This is a chipmuck it is brown it is cute
too. It is my favorite anmunl. I saw
a chipmuck befor at my house,
This chipmuck has little bitty fingers.
And the chipmunch is little to, We are
the chipmunch them and we can
fly like a brid.

Baby girl

Once upon a time, there's a
girl named Laura and she found
out she was going to have a
baby girl. She named the little
baby Kayla. After she had the baby
girl, she still stayed in the hospital.
So, her husband decided to fix a
baby girl room.
   Two days later, she came home
and she cried because it was so
beautiful. There was a rocking chair,
a dresser, and a lamp, window, a crib,
stairs and a rug. That night Laura
decided she would read a story
to the baby and make her fall asleep.
   The next day she went out
to garage sales and she bought the
baby some night gowns, a baby
changer bed, and a new mattess
from Lowes, the store. After Laura
went to Mcdonalds to get some
dinner then, they went to Food
Lion to get baby food.

Story Starter Pictures

Do the following activity with your whole class before introducing the students to the idea of using pictures to help them with topic choices.

Hold up a picture. Have students brainstorm all of the topics that could be written about just by looking at that one picture. Teach students to "dig below the surface." My students were looking at a picture of two birds in a tree with an autumn background. The first thing they all said was, "a story about birds." After that first idea the room was silent. No other topics were volunteered. We then began to "dig below the surface." What else does that picture make you think about?

Friends
Family
The Happiest Time In My Life
Vacations
Sports
Animals
Summer
Swimming
Seasons
Something That Made Me Laugh Out Loud

After brainstorming with the whole class, put six pictures around your room. Number the pictures from one to six. Have students work in groups of 4-5. Each group will need some paper and one student in each group will act as recorder. Each group will begin with a particular picture. The recorder will write the number of the picture on the top of the paper. Set a timer for 1-2 minutes. Students must brainstorm as many topics as they can about the picture.

When the timer goes off, each group takes their list of topics and moves clockwise to the next picture. This procedure is repeated until all groups have visited all of the pictures. The recorder must write the number of each picture on the top of each list of brainstormed ideas.

Bring students back together. Hold up one picture. Each group takes a turn giving a topic suggestion. If any other groups have the same idea, they must all cross it out. Students learn that the more creative they become, chances are no one else will have that idea.

Squiggles

Create a squiggle in the middle of a piece of paper and make a copy for each child. Students take the squiggle, turn it into a picture, and then write about it. Students could write a story or this center could be coordinated with any curriculum area.

Science and Social Studies
Turn your squiggle into:

Something that is living. Tell what it needs to stay alive.

A community. Write about what a community has.

A rural, suburban, or urban setting. Describe what makes it that kind.

A specific season. Describe that season.

Math
Turn your squiggle into:

Any picture. Write word problems.

A picture with three circles and one rectangle. Describe it.

A picture with five things in it.

A picture that displays symmetry. Tell what is symmetrical and why.

Language Arts
Turn your squiggle into:

Something that Frog and Toad liked to do in the story.

The setting of a book. Describe the setting using your senses.

Something that happened in a certain chapter of your book.

The connections you can make to your curriculum are endless!

The following examples range from emergent readers and writers to fluent, proficient readers and writers. The only things that change at this center are the squiggle and topic.

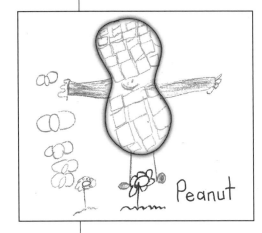

Peanut

snowman

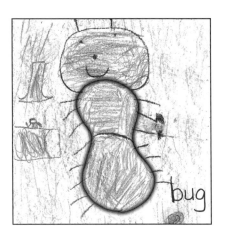

bug

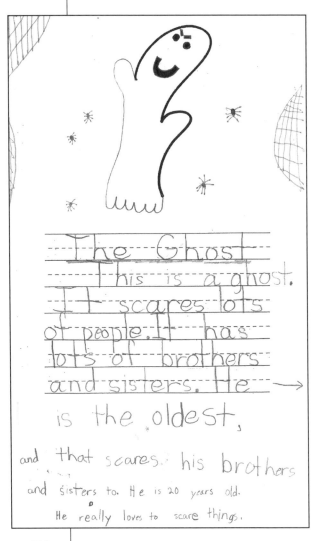

The Ghost
This is a ghost.
It scares lots
of people. It has
lots of brothers
and sisters. He →
is the oldest,
and that scares his brothers
and sisters to. He is 20 years old.
He really loves to scare things.

My squiggle is
a bute. it is big. the bute
is blak.

Assignment: Turn your squiggle into some kind of cycle and write about it.

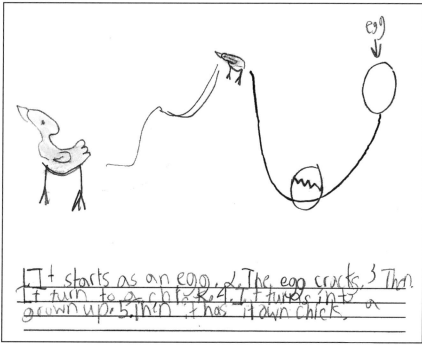

1. It starts as an egg. 2. The egg cracks. 3 Then It turn to a chick. 4. It turns into a grown up. 5. Then it has it own chick.

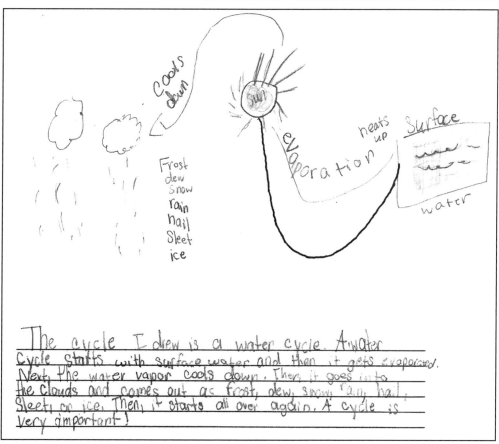

The cycle I drew is a water cycle. A water cycle starts with surface water and then it gets evaporated. Next, the water vapor cools down. Then, it goes into the clouds and comes out as frost, dew, snow, rain, hail, sleet, or ice. Then, it starts all over again. A cycle is very important!

Assignment: Turn your squiggle into something that is part of a state fair and write about it.

This is a pig that won first place. Sometimes in state fairs they have competition with animals that are trained to compete and look good for judges. People go to state fairs to enter there animles to see which one is the best. Lots of people enter animals in contests. Also lots of people around the wold have state fairs.

My squiggle is a stage. Which people come and they have the winners. My squiggle has the top three well-grown pumphins. In my squiggle each pumphin has a stand and a ribbon. Also, their owners are sitting next to them and they are going to bow.

Character Pictures

Students are given the whole character or part of a character from a read-aloud or a book they are reading. You can give students either the character, or part of character, to glue onto a piece of paper. They can place the character anywhere they choose, add scenery, and then write (see *The Adventures of Victor* and *Foodle* examples below). You could also place the characters on a piece of paper and make copies of the whole piece of paper. Students would not need to cut and glue the characters because the characters are already there. They would need to add the scenery and then write (see the *Two Bad Ants* examples on the following page).

They can retell the story or write a new episode.

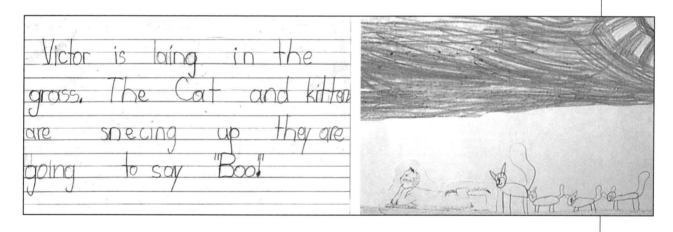

Victor is laing in the grass. The Cat and kitten are sneeing up they are going to say "Boo!"

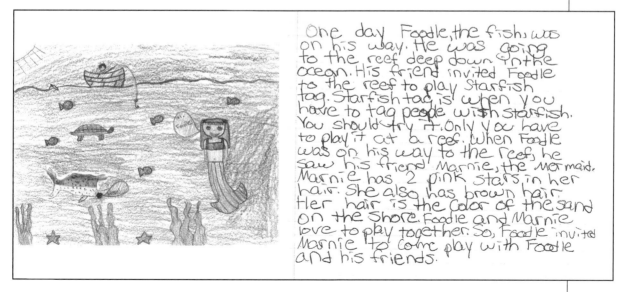

One day Foodle, the fish, was on his way. He was going to the reef deep down in the ocean. His friend invited Foodle to the reef to play starfish tag. Starfish tag is when you have to tag people with starfish. You should try it. Only you have to play it at a reef. When Foodle was on his way to the reef, he saw his friend Marnie, the mermaid. Marnie has 2 pink stars in her hair. She also has brown hair. Her hair is the color of the sand on the shore. Foodle and Marnie love to play together. So, Foodle invited Marnie to come play with Foodle and his friends.

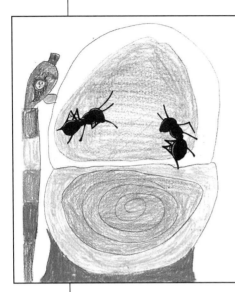

The next day the ants wanted to go home so they went to another room. The ants thought there was a swimming pool. It was really a toilet. The ants climbed and jumped. At that moment a bottle fell on a handle. The ants were in a worlepool! The worlepool ended up to the forest again and the two bad ants went straight home.

The two bad ants are haching roomy in the toy chest. They think the toys are friendly especially the teddy bear. They like him because he is cute and cuddly. Than they fall all the way to the bottom and see a monster toy. They get so scared and climb up on the toys and get out.

The ants stayed for one more day. For the second day they discovered a slime hole just so you know they were really in the living room were there was a big couch. They fell in the hole and a lady spilled juice in the couch. So some coins in the couch. They thought that the coins were gold so they tried to get out. They did and the saw the ants so they brong the gold and went to show it to the queen.

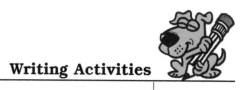

Letters and Notes

Each week put up the name of a student in the classroom. Everyone has to write a letter to that student. Younger children usually write Dear _____, draw a picture and close with From or Love, _____.

Older children are given more direction. They must include three things in the letter.
1. Something they like about the student
2. Something positive they noticed about the student
3. Something they hope to do with the student before the year is over.

Keep these letters and bind each child's letters together. On Valentine's Day students are given a book of letters written to them by classmates.

After we had gone through all of the names in my classroom, this activity became open-ended. Students could write to anyone they wished. They had a difficult time with it being so general and always asked to whom they could write. So each week, for the rest of the school year, I put up a name of someone involved with our school. For example:

the principal	the nurse	the secretary
bus drivers	kitchen cooks	custodians
crossing guards	other teachers	

This is a great place to write thank-you notes and letters. There are so many people who do things for our students and they do not always get acknowledged. This is a time and place where students can thank others for the "little things" that are done to make our lives better. Students really enjoy writing to their teacher. (There are some examples on the following page).

Students can also write as a character from one book writing to a character in another book; or two characters from the same book writing to each other. They can write a letter from themselves to a character in a book. They could write a letter that connects to science and social studies. For example, students could write as Christopher Columbus asking Queen Isabella to supply him ships for his voyage.

The following are some examples of letters students have written.

Dear Mrs. LaPorta,

I can teach you how to draw as good as me.

Dear Mrs. LaPorta,

I lost my crayon box. Scott has the same kind. I'm not saying it's mine I'm just wondering. Because I drew a lion on and his has the same character. And I scribbled on the top and his has it too!

Dear Juan,

I like your soccer skills. You are a fast runner! You are learning English fast! I hope to sit at a table with you!

Sincerely,

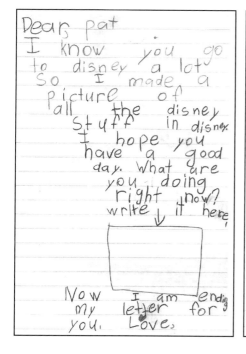

Dear pat
I know you go
to disney a lot
So I made a
picture of
all the disney
stuff in disney.
I hope you
have a good
day. What are
you doing
right now?
write it here

Now I am ending
my letter for
you. Love,

Dear Nate theGreat,
I have read a lot of stories
about your cases. But, I think
you should hire me because
I figured out that little Hex was
in rosamond's basket before you did.
Look at the clues. Little Hex was following
Rosamod to Esmerefa's house and you
weren't paying attention to little
Hex. Rosamond also said that her
basket was heavier than Annie's
basket. They had both been to the
same houses to get candy, that is
why I, Emily the Magnificant, should
be hired by you, Nate the Great.

(P.S.- I wonder if little Hex is
ready to Haunt on Halloween
next year?)

The book *The Jolly Postman,* by Janet and Allan Ahlberg, is a great resource to use with letter writing. This book is about a postman who delivers letters to fairy tale characters. Every other page in the book is an envelope with a letter inside.

Students make their own "envelope book." They take three or four envelopes and staple them together. Students address each envelope and put a note/letter inside.

You could leave this assignment open-ended and not give directions as to what to include in the envelopes. Or make this teacher-directed by giving specific requirements for each envelope; such as a business letter, friendly letter, postcard, advertisement, etc.

Journals

Journals used to be a whole class assignment during a specific time of the day. Instead, journals are now a part of center and assignment time when guided reading groups are meeting. Students decorate a title page for each month. Their title page must include:

Number of days in the month
Holidays
What season the month is in
Five words the month makes you
    think of
Pictures of two things you can do
    during the month
Some famous birthdays

You could have a prompt that students must write about or have students choose their own topics.

Stackable Trays

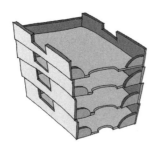

Stackable trays are plastic trays that stack on top of each other. In the trays are "fill-in" sheets for students to complete. Sometimes students have free choice as to which paper they want to do. Other times I assign a specific tray that they must complete first. When they complete the assigned paper they have free choice. This is a great place to put worksheets and workbook pages for students to complete. I usually have five or six trays available for students to choose from.

Wordless Books

Wordless books are great resources to use to get children writing. I had a wealth of wordless books in my classroom that students were not really using, until I made the books manipulative and guided students a bit more. If you have access to a laminator, rip the books apart and send each page through the laminator—yes, it is hard to rip a book apart, but after the first tear it gets easier! Cut the edges so they are even. Punch three holes in each page and tie them together with yarn. Using overhead markers, students can write directly on the pages of the books.

If you do not have a laminator, notebook sheet protectors will also work. (Yes, you still have to rip the book apart.) Cut the edges so they are even and put the pages into the sheet protectors. Most of the sheet protectors already have a strip with the three holes punched out. Put the sheet protectors into a three-ring notebook.

Wordless books are great for students who have difficulty coming up with topics. The hardest part has already been done for students. The topic is already there in a storybook picture form. All students have to do is write what they see. Some students write a description about what they see on each page. Others write stories. Emergent writers will often label things they see in the pictures.

You could incorporate any skill into the writing assignment. You could tell students their writing must include:

      Conversations
      Compound words
      Verbs ending with "ing"
      Words instead of "nice"

Anything you are teaching in grammar, punctuation, editing and revising, language arts skills, etc. can be utilized at this center. The list is endless.

Authors

Students write books and stories. Some students will write a sentence or two about a topic and call it a "story," as shown in the examples below. Others may write more, as shown on the next page.

I have a dog at home. My dog's name is Libby.

I HV A DOG AT HOM. MI DOGS NAM IS LABE.

I have four pets: Cinnamon, Soot, Woody, Spike.

I HAV + PAS

(I have four pets.)

SNAMN
Cinamon

SAK
spike.

S R T
Soot

Y D
woody

King bore pikes flowers.
To day King barewas going.
to his grodin he going.
to his kasatie to go see a sour

I have a dog.
It is a girl.
She well play with you.
She is brown.
She has fure hair.
And she is nice.
And hir name is sky.

He hokid The Bat rog. You
Shud hold The Bat rit in
Basbal. You haf to be god
1. Pick up the bat
2. STUP TO the bas
3. SWIn The Bat

Spending a day in the forest is
an amazing opportunity. The first thing
I saw were trees everywhere. They were tall
and stout. I fell into a tree that was hollow.
I was glad there wasn't a bee hive in the tree.
Beside the trees there were a lot of green
things. There were ferns growing on the ground
with moss growing in-between them. The moss
was all wet and sponge-like. The leaves above
me formed a ceiling like structure with light
glimering through.
Up ahead I could see a pond in the
clearing. It was sparkling in the sunlight. Fish
were jumping up and out of the water. Frogs
were jumping from lilypad to lilypad.
After visiting the pond I saw a snake
slither right by me. I heard the birds chirping. Then
I saw a huge bear. After all of that I was out of
there! But all in all being in the forest is a
pretty good experiance.

The End!

LITERATURE CONNECTIONS

Literary Friends

For Younger Students

Literary Friends are friends from literature that come to visit the classroom. Hang up a picture of a character. The character leaves a letter for the students, asking them to write to him/her. I used a cardboard mailbox and attached the character to the mailbox. Either the teacher writes back or an older grade level class can do the writing. The character stays for about a month, or as long as the interest is there.

Below are examples of letters my students have written to literary friends.

Dear Mouse,
How are you doing? Where do you live? Do you like cookies?
Love, Cormac

DEAR MOUSE HOW ARE YOU DING
WHERE DO YOU LIVE? DO YOU LIKE
COOKIES LOVE CORMAC

To Ping from the book *The Story About Ping* by Majorie Flack.

Dear Ping,
Is it cold where you live?
Love, Krystal

DEAR PING
W
ISITCOELD WERU
LEU
LOVE KRYSTAI

DEAr
PING
WATRDOIN G
LOV
RYAN

Dear Ping,
What are you doing?
Love, Ryan

When you are ready to change the character, do it after school so the students are surprised the next morning. The character that goes away leaves cookies and a drink to say thank you to the students for writing to him/her, and a new character is on the mailbox.

My mom was a first grade teacher for twenty-eight years. She is a fabulous seamstress. She made this Clifford costume for us to use in the classroom. Clifford came to my classroom to personally thank the students for their letters and then he introduced the new literary friend.

Characters that have visited my classroom are The Cat In The Hat, Clifford The Big Red Dog, Max from *Where The Wild Things Are*, Lovable Lyle, and Ping from *The Story About Ping*.

For Older Students

Sometimes students are given prompts for the Literary Friends. Each prompt stays for approximately two weeks. Below are some examples of prompts that have been used.

Write to:

Aunt Sponge and Spiker from *James and the Giant Peach* and tell them how you feel about the way they are treating James.

Attean or Matt from *Sign of the Beaver* and discuss their feelings about life.

Charlotte and Wilbur from *Charlotte's Web* and discuss friendship.

Students can write to one character from another character's point of view. The example below has Frog writing to Toad.

Dear Frog,

Thanks for the advice. Telling me to stop yelling at my plants so they would grow was a good idea. I don't like to be yelled at and neither do the plants. They were afraid when I yelled at them. We'll see you later, Frog. My plants look beautiful!

Sincerely,
Toad.

Story Rewrites and Innovations

Text rewrites and innovations used in your classroom go along with a read-aloud story, a book used during guided reading, or a story from their basal/anthology. Sometimes students are given structures, like the examples below, from *The Grouchy Ladybug*. Other times they use blank paper like the examples on the following page.

We read, <u>The Grouchy Little Ladybug,</u> by Eric Carle.

On ___Saturday___ at ___12:00___
he ___climd up a flovr.___

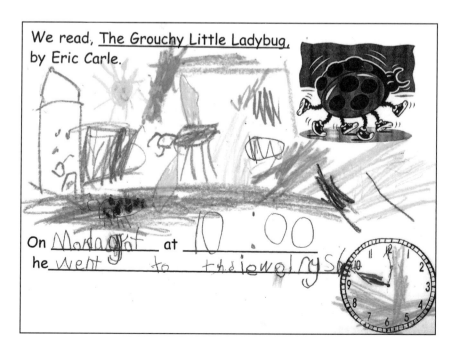

We read, <u>The Grouchy Little Ladybug,</u> by Eric Carle.

On ___Mondgy___ at ___10:00___
he ___went to the jewelry S___

Samples after reading *Fortunately*

Fortunately a little girl named Laura was getting ready to go to her dance recital. Laura loved being a ballerina.

Unfortunately Laura forgot her lucky teddy bear Sam. Laura thought that Sam brought her good luck when she danced.

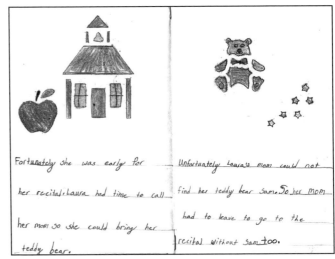

Fortunately she was early for her recital. Laura had time to call her mom so she could bring her teddy bear.

Unfortunately Laura's mom could not find her teddy bear Sam. So her mom had to leave to go to the recital without Sam too.

Samples after reading *Anamalia*

E Eric eats eggs every evening.

Comical Calamari Creating Caricatures

Flipbooks

Flipbooks are made with any sized piece of paper.

First: Take the piece of paper and fold it in half lengthwise.

Next: Fold it in half widthwise.
Then: Fold one last time widthwise.

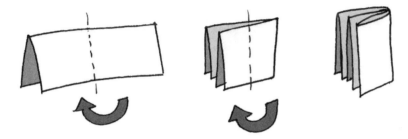

Last: Open the paper. Unfold and cut the top
horizontal fold lines half way down the paper

Flipbooks can have any number of flaps
depending upon how they are folded. They
can be used for a number of different literature
connection activities.

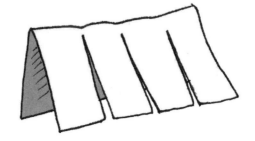

Literature Connections

Sequencing

Students draw and/or write the
sequence of
the story.

inside of
flipbook

Summary

Students draw and/or write a summary of each chapter under the flaps.

Story Elements

Students draw a picture on the top half of the page and write about the story element on
the bottom half of the page.

outside of
flipbook

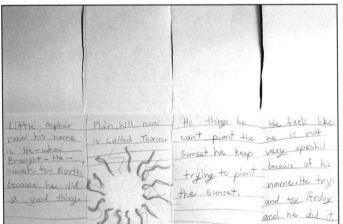

inside of
flipbook

Question Words

Who, What, Where, Why, When, How

Students make their flipbooks into six sections. They write the question words on the outside of the flipbooks. Students tell about these question words in relation to the story and draw pictures under the flaps.

Describing Characters

Students list four words to describe their character on the outside flaps.

They must back up their descriptions with evidence from the story.
They may draw pictures, write down the evidence, or give page numbers
where the evidence is found in the book.

Students' Opinions About the Book

Students write four words that describe their feelings about the book on the outside flaps.

They must back up their opinions with evidence from the story. Students need to tell why they have those opinions.

Cause/Effect

Students write the cause on the outside of the flipbook and the effect on the inside of the book.

This activity works great with Laura Numeroff's books *If You Give A Mouse A Cookie, If You Give A Moose A Muffin*, and *If You Give A Pig A Pancake*.

Main Idea/Supporting Details

Students write the main idea of what they have read on the outside of the flaps. On the inside they write the supporting details.

This works well when students are in chapter books or books that take two or three days to complete.

Fun Facts

There are different ways to organize this research center. Most of the time it is directly related to your science and social studies curriculum. It may also be related to a setting or era from a book that is being read.

Option 1
Students have free choice as to the books they choose and information they write about. They can bring books from home or from the library. The topics are based upon students' choices and interests. Our goal is to give students practice reading and working with expository texts.

Option 2
Students are given a topic they must research. There are a number of books available at varying reading levels for students to use. These texts contain content area text features such as table of contents, index, chapter titles, charts, graphs, etc. We want students using scanning and skimming strategies to locate information. There can be specific questions for students to answer or forms to fill out. For this option, we are not asking students to read the whole text, but to use information to guide them where certain answers can be found. See examples one and two.

One

Textual Support from Book (include page and paragraph)	Similarities to Life Now	Differences to Life Now
warm quilt, snuggle, feather bed	we still use quilts and have beds	we don't have feather beds we have springs, water, pull out beds we have fleece blankets, heated blanket, pillow covers
Bodies snug, Ankles showing, long skirt tug	we still wear skirts	we wear mini-skirts, jeans, camisoles, t-shirts, girls bare legs, we have zippers
gather branches, cold stream bucket	still have fires still use wood, some people still use wells	buy our wood, electric fires running water/pay for it
milk the cow	people still milk cows	we buy our milk
plow the garden	still have gardens	we don't hand plow we use lawn mowers sometimes we pay people to mow our lawn
shearing the sheep	there's still wool clothing	Not a lot of hand sheared clothing
one room cabin	people still go camping and stay in cabins	people don't usually live in cabins we live in heated houses
Spoons w/ tin plates, mugs of leather	we still use mugs, spoons, and plates	there made out of china, glass, metal, and we use forks and knives →

Two

Then - 1870's	Now
1. Wood burning stove	1. microwave oven
2. One room schoolhouse	2. schools with many grades
3. Trundle bed	3. bunk beds
4. 3 per bed	4. one per bed
5. toast	5. pancakes
6. cheese and bread	6. pizza
7. bread, meat	7. sheperds pie, Ham steak, carrots
8. Out to eat zero times	8. Eat out 2 or 3 times
9. girls were dresses home make wool pant	9. jeans
10. steel pans	10. plastic tupperware

Option 3

Students are given a topic they must research. They are given picture books or short stories to read. They gather information from their reading and "show what they have learned." Students may use any writing form they choose. Some like using flipbooks as seen in samples three and four. Some write mini reports as seen in examples five and six.

George Washington was the first president of the United States.

The Thomas Jefferson Memorial was built to honor our third president

The Abraham Lincoln Memorial was built in 1943.

Three

They are black
They can fly
They warmbloded
They born not in eggs

The bat eat little insects
They like to eat insects
and other kind of food

gigantic flying fox
Hoary bat
Vampire bat

Four

The Cheetah

The cheetah is the fastest animal alive. It can go up to 70 miles per hour. But the cheetah can only go short distances. It is known as a hunting leapord. It is usully found in Africa and southern Aisa in grassy lands. They hunt for deer, antalop, and grazzle. They have many spots and a yellowish, gold backround. Thats

The End!

Five

Did you know the fastest snake is probably a Black Mamba? It goes 70 mph, thats for a snake. The Ball Python stays safe by rolling into a ball other snakes do the same. One of the largest snakes is an anaconda if can be 30 feet. The green Tree Python can be yellow or brown but when they lay eggs then it turns green Now you know more about snaks.

Six

Character Portraits

This activity works with many areas of your curriculum: vocabulary development, scanning and skimming, textual support, inferencing, paragraphing, main idea, and supporting details.

Students choose a character from a book they are reading or from a read-aloud. They draw a picture of their character in the middle of a piece of paper. They must choose four words to describe that character. To increase their vocabulary development, students were initially told their words must be two or more syllables. That immediately got rid of words such as nice, good, great, sad, mad, etc. However, some students said, "You know there are some really good one-syllable words like "bold," "curt," and "vain." That is true! So the directions now are that students must choose high-level, meaty words to describe their character. The word should be more than one syllable. However, they may use a one-syllable word if they think it is a strong, powerful word choice. Also, the word they choose cannot be in the book. For example, if the book states that a character is "helpful," students may not use that word. They could go to the thesaurus and find a synonym for helpful, but they may not use a word directly stated in the book.

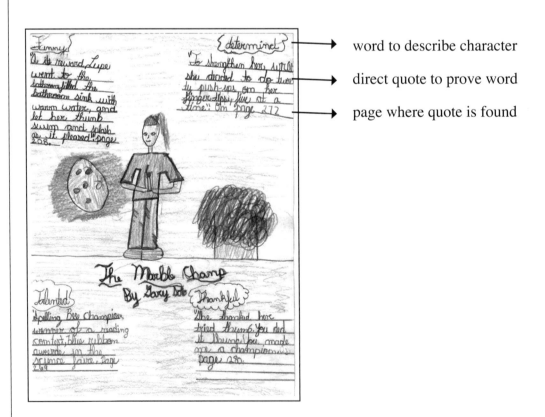

word to describe character

direct quote to prove word

page where quote is found

Students must now go back into their texts and get a direct quote to back-up each word choice. They must give the page and paragraph where the quote is found. This is a great assignment for drawing conclusions. Students are looking at what a character says and does that lead them to their word choices. See the examples below and on the following pages.

Depending upon grade level and students' abilities, a four-paragraph paper can now be written to describe the character. The main idea of each paragraph would be the chosen word followed by supporting details.

Says

Students write quotes from the book of things the character says that reveals his/her character traits and personality. Page and paragraph of where the quote can be found are also written.

Feels

Students write how the character is feeling. They must include page and paragraph that back up why the character is feeling a certain way.

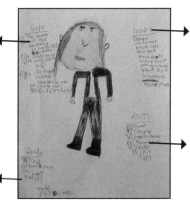

Looks

Students write words to describe the character's physical appearance.

Acts

Students write how the character acts. They must include page and paragraph that prove the character is acting a certain way and why.

Vocabulary Fun

Students are working with vocabulary words from many different sources: their guided reading books and stories, science books, social studies books, read-alouds, news magazines, independent reading materials, etc. Their assignment is to "show what the word means." They can do anything they choose to show that they understand the meaning of the word. The following is a list of ways students can show their understanding of vocabulary.

Give some synonyms
Give some antonyms
Use the word in a sentence about home, school or themselves
Draw a picture
Write the definition in their own words
Make a connection
Tell why the author chose that one particular word and not another

Because students bring such a range of abilities, interests, and personalities to our classrooms, this provides them with many choices to express their knowledge of words and concepts.

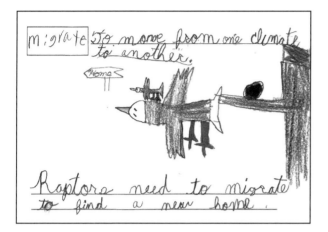

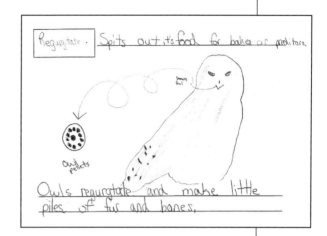

These students made a poem about the word.

The only change at this center are the vocabulary words.

LANGUAGE ARTS

Playing With Words

The following is made from a three-fold presentation board.

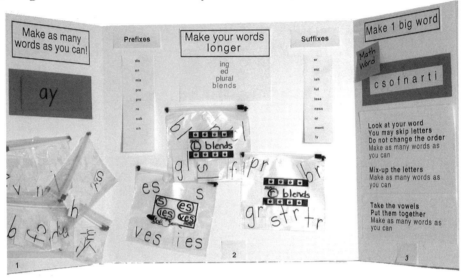

Preparation For Section 1

Fill six small baggies with consonants. Consonants can be written on 1" by 1" graph paper and then run off and put into each bag. Put in extra copies of the popular consonants such as R,S,T, etc. Velcro these baggies to the board.

Write the following along the top of this section: "Make as many words as you can." Laminate a piece of red paper about 3" by 8". Tape it to the board directly under the title. This is where you will write the pattern students are to work with each week.

Place a tub filled with strips of red paper next to the board.

Directions for Section 1

The goal of this section is to have students make as many words as they can with the pattern being studied during the week. The pattern is in red at the top of the board.

Students take a piece of red paper from the margarine tub and copy the pattern that is in red on the board.

They take a baggy of letters off the board. Keeping the red pattern consistent, students make as many word as they can by changing the beginning and ending consonants. They must record all the words they make.

If students get done before work time is over, they can do the following: draw pictures about their words, use the words in sentences, or go on to the second section of the board.

Preparation For Section 2

Fill some small baggies with "add-ons." These can be written on 1" by 1" graph paper and then run off and put into each bag. The following are suggestions for these baggies.

Suffixes	Prefixes	"L" Blends	"R" Blends
ing	pre	bl	br
ed	re	cl	fr
ly	mis	fl	gr

Write the following along the top of this section: "Make your words longer."

Directions for Section 2

The goal of this section is to have students make their words longer. Using the words created in section one, students add suffixes, prefixes, blends, etc.

As you teach different endings, put them on the board for students to practice using. The first endings I usually put up are "ing", "ed", and "s". As students continue to learn more throughout the year, make baggies to Velcro onto the board. For example: "es", change the "y" to "i" and add "es", "er", etc.

If students were working with "ay", and made the word "pay" in section one, then the following changes could be made in section two:

Using the Suffix Baggie
Paying   Pays
Payment   Payer

Using the Prefix Baggie
Prepay

This is just a small sampling of the different ways to play with the word "pay." They must record all the words they make. If students get done before work time is over, they can do the following: draw pictures about their words, use the words in sentences, or go on to the third section of the board.

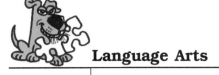

Preparation For Section 3

Write the following along the top of this section: "Make one big word."

Write a scrambled word on red paper for this section. It is always a curriculum word from math, science, or social studies. Place a post-it next to the scrambled word telling what content area it is from.

Place a can filled with strips of 1" graph paper next to the board.

Directions for Section 3

Students take a strip of graph paper. They copy the letters from the red strip on the board onto their graph paper. Students then cut the graph paper apart and unscramble the letters to make one long content word. This activity may become too hard if the scrambled word is not one that they have been working with in the classroom. Putting a post-it near the scrambled word telling what content area it is from is also very supportive for students. For example:

Math Word

r t n o s a f c i

They know it is a math word because of the post-it. First, students unscramble the word and write it on a piece of paper.

fractions

Then students make as many words as they can using any one of the three options on the following page.

Option 1
Look at your word.
You may skip letters.
Do not change the order.
Make as many words as you can.

Fractions

in	tin	fin	fins
at	rat	rats	fat
on	ton	tons	an
fan	fans	ran	act

This is a sampling of the words that can be made.

Option 2
Take the vowels.
Which pairs would go together?
Make as many words as you can.

Fractions

A I O

AI	Students make as many "ai" words as they can.
OA	Students make as many "oa" words as they can.
OI	Students make as many "oi" words as they can.

Option 3
Mix-up the letters.
Make as many words as you can.

F r a c t i o n s

coin	coins	tar	train
rain	rains	star	cart

This is a sampling of the words that can be made.

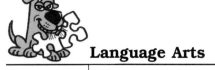

Pull-Throughs and Flip-Overs

To the right is an example of a pull-through. Students pull the strip of paper and make words containing the "ark" pattern.

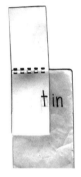

To the left is an example of a flip-over. Students flip over the paper on the left to make words containing the "in" pattern.

Pull-throughs and flip-overs directly coordinate with your phonics and spelling patterns. Students have four tasks with each word they make.

1. Read the word.

2. Write the word.

3. Draw the word.

4. Use the word in a sentence.

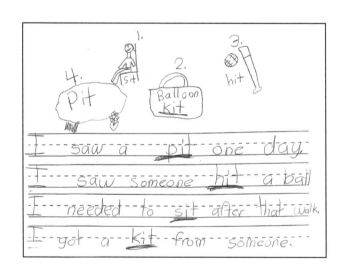

Story paper with the lines on the bottom and plain top for a picture is a great resource to use with this assignment.

Walking the Room

Students can complete this activity either individually or with a partner. Write vowel patterns, blends, etc. on post-it notes and place on clipboards.

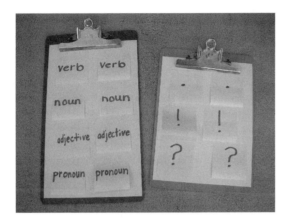

The first time students walk the room they place the notes on words that contain the pattern, blend, rule, etc. The second time students walk the room they take off the post-it notes and copy the sentences in which the words were found.

Students then go back to their seats and use each word in their own sentences.

Extensions
Any of the following can be put on post-its for students to find around the room.

Letters of the Alphabet
Sight Words
Contractions
Plurals
Words with "ing" ending
Quotation Marks
Parts of speech: nouns, verbs, adjectives, adverbs
Capital Letters
Color Words

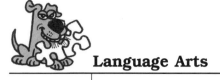

Listening Station

The listening center provides opportunities for independent listening activities. After my students listened to a story, I always had a fill-in sheet for them to complete. The worksheet asked questions about different story elements. Students did a rather poor job filling in the sheets. They would often write: "I liked it" or "It was nice." I realized the sheets were too cumbersome and too general. Students also stated that they did not like having to fill out the same form each week after listening to a story.

I now take one story element each week and use it as a focus in the listening center. There is no fill-in available for students. Each week, depending upon the focus, students have activities from which to choose. The following are activities students can do at the listening center as you concentrate on different story elements.

Follow-Up Activities With Story Elements
Answers can be drawn, written, or a combination of the two.

Characters
Draw the character.
Make a Venn diagram comparing and contrasting you and a character.
What problems did the character have and how did they get solved?
Describe the character.
What is your opinion of the character?
Do you know anyone like the character?
Make a mobile about the character.

Problem/Solution
What problems are the characters facing?
Have you ever had those problems or know someone who has?
What are two solutions you would suggest to solve the character's problems?
How were the problems solved in the story?

Setting
Draw the setting
Describe the setting with your senses. What would you hear? See? Smell? Touch? Taste?
What places do you know that are like the story's setting?
What places do you know that are the opposite of the story's setting?
Create a new setting for the story. How might the story change because of the new setting?

New Endings or New Adventures

Create a new ending to the story.

Create another chapter.

Give the characters another adventure that includes you.

Write a new story about the characters.

Opinions

What is your favorite part? Why?

What didn't you like about the story? Why?

Create a new book cover.

Why should someone read or listen to this story?

Create a book review.

Beginning, Middle, and End or Summary

Draw pictures of the beginning, middle, end.

Write about the beginning, middle, end.

Make an event map of first, next, then, last.

Other Fun Options For Students

Listen to:

    Nature Sounds

    Animal Sounds

    Songs

    Music

Record different people in the school reading a story.

Record parents reading and children saying their favorite part.

Record your read-alouds and their discussions.

Pocket Chart

Pocket charts are great resources for students to practice different curriculum topics and skills. There are many different kinds of pocket charts available. You could change the kind of pocket chart each month to give this center a new look. Some of the things students can do are match, sort, classify, compare and contrast, create, and sequence.

Student can:
Match names to faces
Make complete sentences
Work with punctuation marks
Match rhyming words
Make as many words as they can out of a given pattern
Match contractions to the two words which make up the contraction
Work with making words plural
Categorize words into different parts of speech
Work with noun/verb agreement
Sequence a story, poem, or steps in a process
Etcetera!

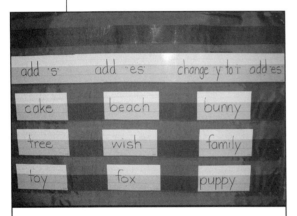

Students are working with rules to make words plural.

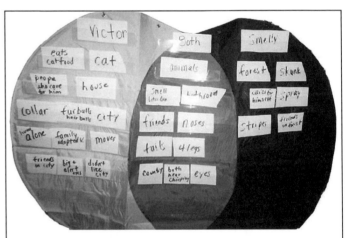

Students are comparing and contrasting Victor and Smelly, two characters from the book *The Adventures of Victor.*

You could also work with your science and social studies curriculum. Students can match states to capitals or vocabulary words to their definitions. They could categorize living things vs. nonliving things or warm-blooded animals vs. cold-blooded animals. The list is endless.

I Can Use It

Have a container of pictures available for students to use. Pictures can come from magazines, calendars, post cards, greeting cards, posters, photographs, and book jackets. Students choose a picture. They apply and utilize whatever curriculum area is being studied to the picture. For example, if you are working with contractions, students would describe their pictures with sentences that included contractions. If you are working with dialogue, students would write conversations between two things in their pictures. Below is an example of a student working with different kinds or sentences.

I saw an elephant at the zoo.
Have you seen an elephant?
Look at that elephant!

You can tie almost any area of your reading and writing skills into this center.

For example:
Parts of speech: nouns, verbs, adjectives, adverbs, pronouns, and prepositions
Contractions
Compound words
Words ending with "ing"
Words that are plural
     Make this more challenging by having students categorize based on the rules for making words plural
Anything to coordinate with your spelling and phonics curriculum

The list is endless! Anything students are learning, you want them to apply and utilize in their writing.

SIGHT VOCABULARY

Find It and Mark It Again and Again

Have students work with a sight word. Using any book, they need to find and mark the word every time it appears in the text. Depending on abilities, students can work with just one word or up to four words. The following items can be used to mark the words.

Highlighter Tape
The first time through the book students mark the sight word every time it appears. The second time through the book students read the book and take off the tape as they come to the word. See page 29 for information about how to use highlighter tape.

Post-Its
Students put a post-it under the word every time they see it.

Arrows
Arrows are like highlighter tape because they can be reused. Arrows can be found at most office supply stores. Store these on strips of laminated paper like the highlighter tape.

Wikki Stixs
These are colored, flexible, waxy sticks that are reusable. Students shape them into circles to circle the words or leave them in strips to underline the words. These can be stored in a margarine tub.

Write a Sentence

Use the books *Look-Alikes*, *Look-Alikes Jr.*, *Look-Alikes Christmas*, and *Look-Alikes Around the World* by Joan Steiner to set up and organize this activity. The pictures in these four books are made from household objects and items. For example, the roof of a house is really a book. The chimney is made of dog bones. The trees are broccoli. The porch is made out of birthday candles. They are clever and motivating books. Put one copy of a book in an area. Clothespin the book open to the pages you want your students to use. Give them a different prompt each week. The prompt is a sentence that contains high frequency words. It should be no longer than four words. Some examples of prompts I've used are:

Look at the ___.
I see a ___.
I see the ___.
Here is a ___.
Here is the ___.
I saw a ___.
There is a ___.
I found a ___.
It was a ___.

You can make the prompts harder for those who want some challenges. For example:

I found a ___ used as a ___.
This is a ___ used for a ___.
You could have used a ___ instead of a ___.
You really wouldn't find a ___ used as a ___.
I noticed a ___ used for a ___.

This could also be used as a dictionary center. Students need to check the words they have independently written.

Going, Going, Gone

Students can work with a partner or in a small group. They need to use a large classroom blackboard or a small portable chalkboard. One child takes a damp sponge and writes a sight word on the board. The other students have to say and spell the word as many times as they can before it disappears. When it finally disappears the word is rewritten on the board with chalk and students correct their work.

You could keep different containers of words to differentiate this activity based on students' needs. There could be a container of words that coordinate with each guided reading group.

If students are working with partners, they could each have their own set of words on ringed index cards.

Clay or Playdough

Students make the word(s) out of clay or playdough at least three times. Have them leave their words in a tray for you to check. Use styrofoam trays that contained family-sized portions of meat from the grocery store. After students have made their word(s) at least three times, they need to write them in sentences. They could have free play with the playdough or clay. You could also use pipe cleaners.

Sand or Salt Trays

Using large styrofoam trays, fill some with sand or salt. Students write sight words in the sand or salt, and then write them with paper and pencil. Place the trays in a plastic tub to help contain the salt and sand.

Plastic Letters

Have the sight words you want students to work with listed on a piece of paper. Also have those words used in sentences for students to see and read. This helps students see the word in isolation as well as in context. Students need to take the plastic letters, make the words, and then write them. They could illustrate the sentences if time allows.

Arty Words

Most students like using anything other then a pencil! At this center students play with their sight words using:

Gel pens
Highlighters
Glitter pens
Stamps
Stencils
Markers
Crayons
Whiteboards
Blackboards
Watercolors and paintbrushes
Sponge paintings

Create It

Have the sight words that students need practice with already written on paper. Students trace each letter with glue and put on pasta, beans, pom poms, string, scrap pieces of paper, cotton balls, beads, buttons, etc.

All of these activities are also great for older students to use to help them with troublesome spelling words.

Sentence Cubes

In addition to sight words, this assignment also reinforces sentence structure and punctuation. Make four cubes using the pattern on page 155. On each cube write the following words or use your own ideas.

Cube #1	Cube #2	Cube #3	Cube #4
My	dog	walked	to the store.
His	mom	went	home.
Their	dad	drove	to the beach.
Our	cat	rode	to the park.
Her	friend	came	to school.
Your	brother	raced	to the mall.

Cube #1 has pronouns.

Cube # 2 has any animal name, family member name, or the word "friend".

Cube #3 has verbs.

Cube #4 has places.

The assignment is to roll the cubes, write the sentences and then illustrate. Students usually roll the cubes a couple of times before they write the sentences. Students should write the four sentences before beginning their drawings.

To make this more challenging, make some blank cubes. Students have to insert the blank cubes into the sentence to make the sentences longer. They need to add adjectives, adverbs, prepositional phrases, etc.

Below are two examples:

My friend skipped to the beach.

①Our dad drove to school. Our friendly dad drove us to the pivet school. ②Her brother went home. Her older brother went home on the bus in the rain ③ Our mom came to the store Our mom came in a car to the store. ④ His mom drove to the beach. His mom drove to the beach in the summer to get tan.

ADDITIONAL ACTIVITIES

Newspaper Detectives

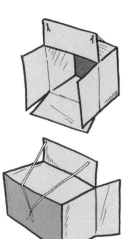

Take a box and cover it with newspaper. Ask three or four students to volunteer for this job. They need to cut out different parts of the newspaper and glue them until the whole box is covered.

Punch two holes in a flap of the box. Tie a long piece of yarn to each hole. Put a brad on the back of the box. When you set up the box, pull the top up and attach both pieces of yarn to the brad. You have created a flap that will stand up. This is where you can put your focus skills or directions for the week. Put several newspapers in the box.

Below are two photos that show how the boxes can be used with younger and older students. The left photo is a newspaper box used in first grade. Students use the newspapers to find words they recognize which begin with the letter "A". Students cut out the words, glue them on a piece of paper, and then use the words in sentences.

The box on the right can be used with fourth graders as they explore the difference between fact and opinion. Students read an article and write down the title on a piece of paper. They make a "T" chart and write down statements in the correct category: fact or opinion. See page 158 for a reproducible that students can use.

Morning Message

For Younger Students

Morning messages can be used over and over again all week for students to practice reading and writing. Each morning, write a letter/message on chart paper to the students. A first or second grade example might look like the following:

> Dear Students,
>
> > Good morning. I missed you this weekend.
> > We have library this afternoon.
> >
> > Love,
> >
> > Miss Pavelka

You will need a piece of clear plastic large enough to cover the letter. Run your laminating machine with nothing in it to get a large sheet of clear plastic. If you do not have access to a laminator, then clear contact paper will also work. Put the sticky sides together to create a large sheet of plastic.

Each morning the students work as a class with the morning message; circling words they know and working with other reading and writing strategies. By putting the clear plastic over the chart paper, the letter can be used over and over again because it is not being written on. The writing, circling, etc. is done on the plastic which can be wiped off.

The letter is then placed at a morning message station. Students place the plastic over the messages and manipulate and play with the text. They often play "school." One is the teacher and tells the other students what to do with the letter. Children circle words they know, change the text, add descriptive words, etc.

For Older Students

A third grade letter might look like the following:

> Dear Third Graders:
>
> I missed you this weekend.
> Saturday I shopped and watched a movie.
> Yesterday I baked cookies and helped some friends.
> Today we go to art at 11:15.
>
> Love,
>
> Miss Pavelka

Letters to older students contain many examples of skills that they have been working on in the classroom. The above letter has words with the "ed" ending: missed, shopped, watched, backed, and helped.

Your morning messages are not one-shot deals anymore. They are used over and over again, which builds sight word acquisition as well as fluency.

A discussion should follow about the "ed" ending. One of the words in the letter had its last consonant doubled before the "ed" ending. One word dropped the final "e" before the "ed" ending. Some of the words stayed the same; just an "ed" was added. At the center students would write messages that contained words with "ed" endings. Many times students have memorized the rules and patterns. They can tell the answer by rote, but when writing, they fail to apply the correct information. Using morning messages written to the students has more meaning and carries over into their daily written work rather than arbitrary sentences, which have no connections to students' lives.

This is also a great time to work with editing and revising. Your letter could have mistakes that students have to find and fix.

Mobiles

Mobiles are made using twigs and paper. Students bring the twigs in from recess. They should not be longer than 12".

Using paper strips of any size and color, students wrap the strips around the twigs and staple or tape them down.

While working with teachers, we brainstormed and created samples of mobiles for our classrooms. Below are some examples of our creations.

Mobiles can be used for all curriculum areas. Students can use magazine pictures and glue them on the strips. They can draw and/or write on the strips.

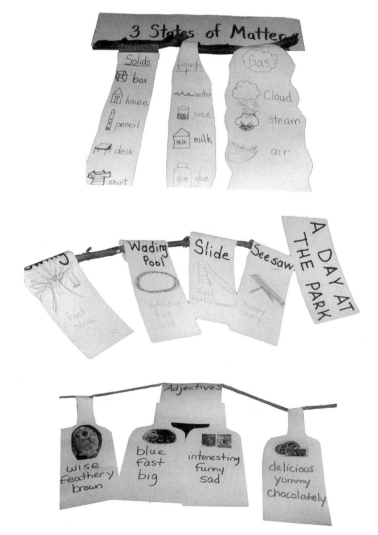

Find It In A Book

This activity usually corresponds with your language arts curriculum for the week. Using highlighter tape, students find examples of the skills they have been taught during the week. Below are examples of some curriculum areas and their extensions.

Three Types of Sentences
Students can find and highlight:
> one sentence that ends with a period,
> one sentence that ends with an exclamation mark,
> one sentence that ends with a question mark.

They need to write each sentence and tell why it uses that specific punctuation mark. Flipbooks are great recording sheets for this activity. On the outside flap students write the punctuation mark. On the top, inside flap the students write what kind of mark it is and then copy the sentence from their books. On the bottom, inside flap they tell why that mark was used.

Quotation Marks
Students can highlight everything that a character says. After finding all of the dialogue, have them write three original sentences that they think the character might say.

Capital Letters
Students find and highlight words that begin with capital letters. After finding words, they need to record and categorize them in a flipbook. On the outside of the flipbook, students put the rule for capitalizing. For example: names of people, states, cities, streets, etc. On the inside they write the examples that were found in their books.

Words Instead of Said.
Find, highlight, and record synonyms for the word "said."

Some examples of other things to find and work with are:
> Parts of speech: nouns, verbs, adjectives, adverbs, pronouns, etc.
> Contractions
> Compound words
> Words ending with "ing"
> Words that are plural
> Cause and effect

The list is endless! Anything students are learning, you want them to find examples in their books. These assignments allow students to actually see the skills embedded in context. It works well with most of our language arts skills.

Playing with Poems

This center coordinates with poems that are introduced whole class, usually during a shared reading time. Introduce one to two poems each week. After you introduce each poem, make a copy, and put it in a protective sleeve and then into a three-ring binder. Have two or three binders available so you have enough for several children. Students usually work together at this center, so if you have three binders, then six students can be working. There are many activities to do at this center.

Students read the poems from the notebook together. They either read chorally or take turns reading.

All of the poems that are in the notebook are also photocopied so that students each have their own copy. They can illustrate the poems.

Make copies of the poem but leave out certain words to make a cloze activity. Students fill in the missing words.

Instead of giving students their own photocopy of the poems, have students copy a favorite poem each week.

There is a tub of poetry books that students can choose to read.

Have students find different patterns that are being studied in your phonics and spelling curriculum.

Students can write their own poems based on the kind of poem that is being studied. Some forms students have studied and worked with are haiku, cinquain, acrostic, concrete, limerick, tanka, ABC, shape, and name.

Compare and Contrast

This center can be used two different ways.

Option 1
Students can compare and contrast concepts and topics that are a part of your curriculum.

<u>Science and Social Studies</u>
Living vs. non-living, landforms, different kinds of communities, animals

<u>Math</u>
Shapes, measurement, numbers

<u>Language Arts</u>
Words: letters, syllables, parts of speech, alphabetical order
Books: characters, settings, problem/solution

Option 2
Students could compare and contrast different items.
Pictures: magazine, post cards, greeting cards, calendars, photocopied papers
Photos
Objects: buttons, marbles, etc

This child compared and contrasted:
> A taco and burrito
> A piano and computer
> A pencil and pen

This child took all the words from the book *The Adventures of Victor* and categorized them in the following ways:
> Words that were names of characters
> Safety words
> Words that described the bunny
> City words
> Feeling words
> Country words
> Words with the same letters (o)

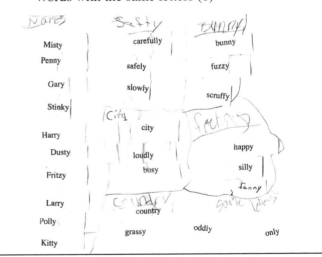

Question Center

This center allows students to ponder their own and others' questions, make connections, and draw conclusions. Have a tub of pictures available for students to use. You could use magazines, calendars, greeting cards, post cards, advertisements, posters, etc.

There are usually two kinds of questions students will write. They will ask questions that are not necessarily thought provoking, but some conclusions must be drawn before they can be answered. For example, when using a picture of a doctor some of their questions may be:

> What is her occupation?
> Where does she work?
> What items does she need to do her job?
> When would you see this person?
> Why is she dressed that way?

Some other question students asked were more opinion based and made them think about their experiences in life.

How do you feel when you have to see a doctor?
When is the last time you've had an experience with a doctor?
What kind of personality do you think this doctor has?

I wonder questions are great for this center.

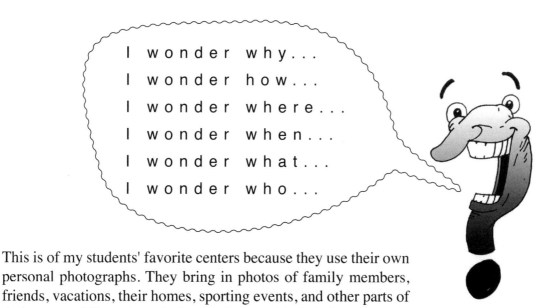

I wonder why...
I wonder how...
I wonder where...
I wonder when...
I wonder what...
I wonder who...

This is of my students' favorite centers because they use their own personal photographs. They bring in photos of family members, friends, vacations, their homes, sporting events, and other parts of their personal lives. A pet is the number one kind of photo brought to this center.

Students are so creative. They wanted this to be a "comic book question" center. They put some of the photos together and wrote comic books. The only text and dialogue, though, could be questions. After students made the comics, more questions were generated. See the example below.

Hey, where is my hammer?

Juneau, did you take his hammer?

If I pretend I don't hear them, do you think this problem will go away?

Hey Sitka, did you look over there?

Why on earth would my hammer be over there on the table?

Juneau, are you going to try and help him find his hammer? Why did I accept this boss job? Is there ever going to be a day where these two aren't arguing?

Don't you think I looked carefully?

Did you look carefully? If I find it, what will you give me?

Do you two see who is coming? Do you think you could get your tools together so just once we will be ready on time? Do you two know how late we are?

Based on the dialogue, do you think the "boss man" is a good leader? Why or why not?
Would you want this crew working for you? Why or why not?
Do you think Juneau and Sitka are friends?
What connection can you make to this scenario?

Part 3

Putting It All Together

FORMING THE ASSIGNMENT GROUPS

Try to have a wide range of abilities and personalities in each group. For example, each group may have:

> a child who has difficulties with attention and behavior
> a calm child who has no difficulties with attention and behavior
> a proficient reader
> a struggling reader

You want these groups to be diverse in both personalities and learning styles.

Students are in two groups:
a reading group and a center/work group.

Guided reading groups are homogeneous groups of students working together with the teacher in a guided reading format or independently as a background group (see Part One). These are students who are reading at approximately the same level.

Assignment groups are heterogeneous groups of students working alone or with each other as assignments and/or centers are being completed.

These groups change membership only twice a year. You want to create a group of students that learns how to work together. They support each other in both academic and social areas. Once they have established a working relationship, you don't want to change them and begin the process all over. You may find, when you first establish the groups, minor adjustments need to be made.

Each group has a color name: red, blue, green, yellow, etc. The teacher assigns each group a color.

Take your guided reading groups and mix them together to form the assignment groups.

First, make a list of your students in each guided reading group. The list on the following page will be used as an example as we go through these next steps.

A (Seals)	Erik	Michaela	Maria	Yarilis		
B (Whales)	Jamal	Soleil	Lauren	Dalisha		
C (Dolphins)	Nathan	Ivan	Henry	Axel	Malik	Carlos
D (Pirates)	Joseph	Savannah	Page	Caleb	Chen	
E (Starfish)	Marcus	Kate	Tammie	Suleima	Jacob	Janet

Next, decide how to mix the students so each center/work group has students from each guided reading group. You can put students together in groups of two, three, four, five, or six. It does not matter how many students you have in each group. Remember from Part 1 that each guided reading group's name is based on your science or social studies topics. Each center/work group is named a color.

Start by taking a crayon (red for example) and color over Erik's name (the first student on your list.) Now look at the Whales. Decide who in the Whale group would be a good match to put in Erik's group and color over that name. Then look at the Dolphin group and decide who would be a good match to put with Erik and Lauren and color over that name. Continue in this fashion as you work through the rest of the guided reading groups. The shaded names represent the Red group.

A (Seals)	Erik	Michaela	Maria	Yarilis		
B (Whales)	Jamal	Soleil	Lauren	Dalisha		
C (Dolphins)	Nathan	Ivan	Henry	Axel	Malik	Carlos
D (Pirates)	Joseph	Savannah	Page	Caleb	Chen	
E (Starfish)	Marcus	Kate	Tammie	Suleima	Jacob	Janet

In the scenario above, no one was chosen from the Pirates group because none of those students would be a good match for the group being formed. So there are four students in the Red group (the shaded names).

Take a different color (blue for example) and color over Michaela's name (the second student on your list.) Now look at the Whales. Decide who in the Whale group would be a good match to put in Michaela's group and color over that child's name. Then look at the Dolphin group and decide who would be a good match to put with Michaela and Dalisha and color over that name. Continue in this fashion as you work through the rest of the guided reading groups. The names shaded with a diagonal represent the Blue group. There are four members in the Blue group.

A (Seals)	Erik	Michaela	Maria	Yarilis	
B (Whales)	Jamal	Soleil	Lauren	Dalisha	
C (Dolphins)	Nathan	Ivan	Henry	Axel	Malik	Carlos
D (Pirates)	Joseph	Savannah	Page	Caleb	Chen
E (Starfish)	Marcus	Kate	Tammie	Suleima	Jacob	Janet

Continue in this fashion until you have colored over everyone's name. You can now see the dynamics of the groups you have made. There may be times when you choose two students from the same guided reading group to be in the same color group. That is fine.

Let's look at our example and look at it in detail.

A (Seals)	Erik	Michaela	Maria	Yarilis	
B (Whales)	Jamal	Soleil	Lauren	Dalisha	
C (Dolphins)	Nathan	Ivan	Henry	Axel	Malik	Carlos
D (Pirates)	Joseph	Savannah	Page	Caleb	Chen
E (Starfish)	Marcus	Kate	Tammie	Suleima	Jacob	Janet

This scenario has seven center/work groups:

Red has four members.
Blue has four members
Green has four members
Yellow has two members
Purple has four members
Orange has four members.
Brown has three members.

This organization is very flexible. It does not matter how many center/work groups you have and how many members make up each group. Whatever you do will work. It depends on how many students you want working together and the dynamics of each group. Students have to remember the names of their reading groups (always a content area name that they gave themselves) and a color.

ORGANIZING THE ROTATION CHART

You need two pieces of posterboard, one white and one of a light color. Use the light colored piece of posterboard as the background. Take the white piece of posterboard and cut out a large circle (wheel). Using a magic marker, divide the wheel into eight centers. Color each section of the wheel a different color. Laminate the wheel.

Using a paper fastener, attach the wheel to the middle of the background posterboard. Continue the lines that divide the wheel onto the background posterboard with magic marker. See the example below (remember your wheel sections are different colors. The example below is shown in black and white).

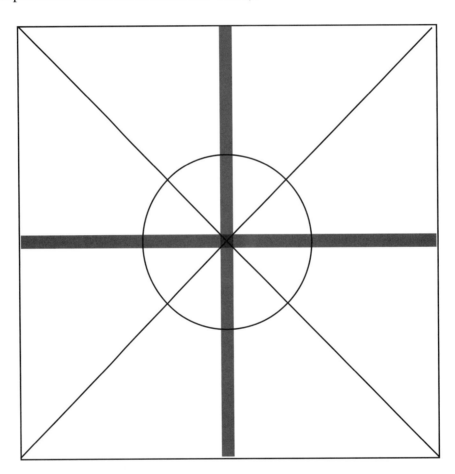

When using eight centers you can work with quadrants. Notice, in the example above and on the following page, the quadrants are very easy to see. My mistake was to not make the quadrants themselves bold enough. I now use three-inch red ribbon to make the quadrants show. Students can't miss seeing them.

Names of the students will be written in each color section of the wheel. The background sections are for writing the different assignments and/or centers. The same names from the Forming the Assignment Groups section (pages 126-129) are also being used here.

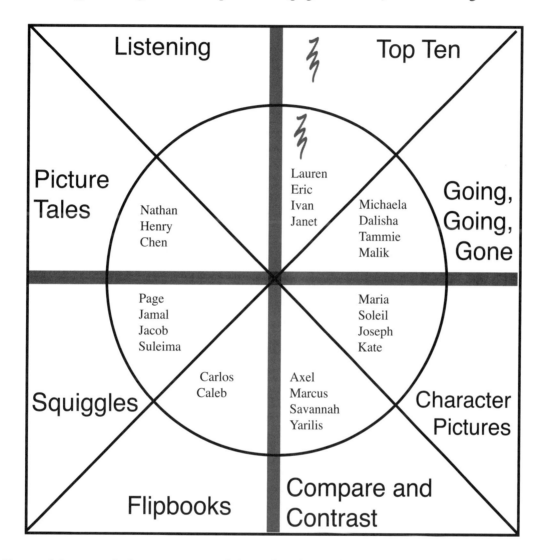

Put a sticker, symbol, etc., on one of the colored wheel sections and on one of the center assignments. In the above example, a lightning bolt is placed on the Top Ten section and the brown section of the wheel. Begin the wheel rotation with the two lightning bolts aligned together. As you turn the wheel the symbols become unaligned. When the lightening bolts realign, your students have completed one full rotation of centers.

As you organize your chart, be aware of the order of the centers. Try not to put two writing centers/activities next to each other, or two easier centers/activities next to each other.

Using the Rotation Chart

Students get only two directions daily: Start on your color. Stay in your quadrant. That's it! Most students know to which color group they are assigned. If they do not remember, they can look for their names on the chart. Whichever color is next to their name is the first assignment they will complete. So looking at the chart on the previous page, Eric, Lauren, Ivan, and Janet will begin working at Top Ten. Michaela, Dalisha, Tammie, and Malik will begin working at Going, Going, Gone. When it is time to visit the second assignment of the day, Eric, Lauren, Ivan, and Janet will work with Going, Going, Gone. Michaela, Dalisha, Tammie, and Malik will work with Top Ten. So students start on their color for the first assignment and then stay in their quadrant for the second assignment.

When students ask the questions:

Where do I go?

What am I supposed to do?

The answer is: start on your color.
Stay in your quadrant.

Each morning the wheel moves one quadrant. It takes four days for the wheel to make a complete turn. Students work on assignments from Monday through Thursday. On Friday, students have time to correct their work and/or finish their work. Students who were absent have time to complete some of the missed work. Students who have completed the assignments have time to extend their work.

All students will have two assignments to work on and one group experience (either guided reading or background group). The difference is the order of their routines.

There are three options that students may have during the hour block, each taking approximately twenty minutes.

Students may:
First work on an assignment, then work on a second assignment, and finally have a small group experience

First work on an assignment, then have a small group experience, and finally work on a second assignment,

First have a small group experience, then work on an assignment, and finally work on a second assignment,

Not all students in a color group will be working on the same assignment at the same time. Everyone in the same color group will complete the same assignments; just at different times depending on when they are called to meet with the teacher or in the background group.

GETTING STARTED STEP BY STEP

Week I

Goals: Students learn their color groups.
Introduce two assignments from Part 2.

Color Groups

Hang up your *blank* rotation chart. Do not have any names or centers written on it. Have students sit so they can easily see the rotation wheel. Write the names of students onto the colored sections as they watch you (see page 126 for information on how to establish the groups).

Engage in quick activities all week long to help students learn their group colors. Have students line up for lunch, recess, art, music, library, gym, etc. by colors. Throughout the day ask different colored groups to do certain tasks. For example:

"Blue group, stand up."
"Green group, wave at me."
"Red group, put your hands in the air."

Assignments

Introduce two assignments to the students. Spend two days on each assignment and review both on Friday. Introduce these assignments to your whole class. Students do not know that these assignments will eventually be centers. Your goal is to teach these activities so that students will be able to work independently on them while you are with a guided reading group.

After introducing an assignment, have students sit in their color groups to complete the task. As they are working, you will be monitoring groups looking for strengths and weaknesses. Try not to answer any questions that may arise. Lead students to ask each other for help and clarification of directions. By having them work in their color groups, you will see how they interact and whether or not you need to do some movement of membership.

On Friday, write the names of the two assignments on the rotation chart. After week one, your chart may look like this:

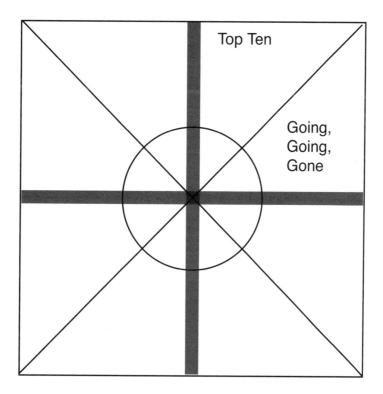

If students ask why you are writing the assignments on the chart, tell them they will find out soon!

Week II

Goals: Students continue learning their color groups.
Introduce two more assignments from Part 2.

Color Groups

Continue working with students' knowledge of their color groups. Engage in quick activities all week long to help students learn the colors of their groups. Have students line up for lunch, recess, art, music, library, gym, etc. by colors. This week you want to introduce movement to the groups. Throughout the week ask different colored groups to quickly and quietly walk to certain places in the classroom. For example:

"Blue group, walk quickly and quietly to the window."
"Green group, go quickly and quietly to the back of the room."
"Red group, walk quickly and quietly to the tall bookcase."

Your goal is to help students get from their desks or tables to certain places in the room in a quiet manner and as quickly as possible. This is really practice for going to centers.

Assignments

Introduce two more assignments from Part 2 to students. Follow the same format as week one:

       introduce activities to the whole class,
       spend two days on each assignment,
       monitor groups for strengths, weaknesses, and possible group changes,
       guide students to ask each other for help and clarification,
       review both assignments on Friday.

On Friday, write the names of the two learned center activities on the wheel rotation chart. After week two, your chart may look like this:

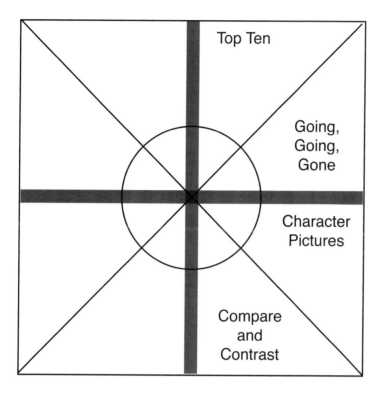

If students ask why you are writing the assignments on the chart, tell them they will find out next week!

Week III

Goals: Students learn how to use the rotation chart.
Introduce two more assignments from Part 2.

Color Groups and Rotation Chart

Students should now know what color groups they belong to. This week, you want to introduce the rotation chart. Have students find their colors on the wheel and then look at the activity that is next to their color. Rotate the wheel and have students find their color and the new assignment that is next to their color. Groups with no activity next to their color should be able to identify, "there is no activity by my color."

Turn the wheel at different times of the day and practice. For example, ask the group who would be working with the squiggle to stand up. Ask the blue group to tell what assignment is next to their color, etc.

Review directions to the assignments that are written on the chart.

Assignments

Introduce two more assignments from Part 2 to students. Follow the same format as weeks one and two.

Write the names of the two learned center activities on the wheel rotation chart. After week three, your chart will be filled in and may look like this:

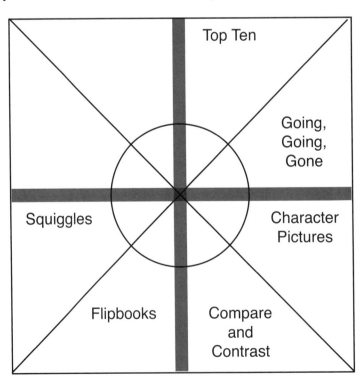

Week IV

Goals: Introduce two more assignments from Part 2.
Students read and apply the rotation chart.

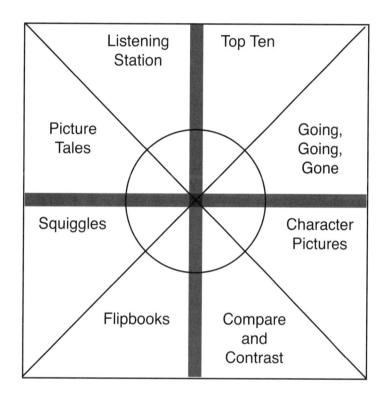

Walk the room with your students, setting up the various centers and assignment stations. Students should help decide where directions are displayed, where materials are kept, etc.

Most of the activities in Part 2 can be set up as either centers where students work together or as independent seat work.

COORDINATING ASSIGNMENT GROUPS
WITH GUIDED READING GROUPS

Preparation

Make two signs. Take a piece of 9" by 12" white construction paper and laminate it. Take a second piece of 9" by 12" white construction paper, draw a large red arrow on it, and laminate.

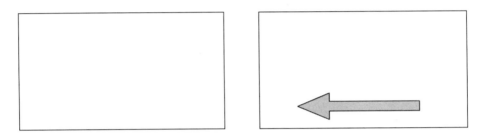

Practice with Students

On the blank laminated paper, use a water soluble, overhead marker to write the name of a guided reading group that you want to meet with. For example: hold up the sign below while you ask the Whales to meet with you at the guided reading table.

Whales

After the Whales come to you, the remaining students look at the rotation chart, find their colors, and go to the corresponding centers. When students have completed this task, ask them to sit down.

Hold up the sign again with a different guided reading group's name. For example: hold up the sign below while you ask the Sharks to meet you at the guided reading table.

Sharks

After the Sharks come to you, ask the remaining students to look at the chart, find their colors, and go to the corresponding centers. When students have done this task, ask them to sit down. Continue this procedure until all guided reading groups have practiced coming to you while the rest of the class find their assignments.

You are not taking guided reading groups for instruction and students are not actually doing the center/work assignments. Students are practicing slow and quiet movement to centers or to you for instruction.

COORDINATING ASSIGNMENT GROUPS WITH GUIDED READING GROUPS AND BACKGROUND GROUPS

Background groups are not explained whole class. During the first five minutes that each guided reading group meets, begin setting up and explaining background group tasks. Organize the box of reading materials with students. Make the highlighter tape cards and index cards with students. Have students help you organize and set up the box as much as possible. The more involved they are in the foundation, the greater their ability to understand the given tasks and complete them independently.

Practice the Reader of the Day activities, sitting on the circles, reading silently, etc. When you think students are ready to work independently as a background group, put them in the background and observe instead of taking them for a guided reading lesson.

When all groups understand background group assignments and responsibilities, spend a couple of days practicing the movement of all three groups: guided reading groups, assignment groups, and background groups. Follow the same procedure as in week four. Now you will need both pieces of laminated paper; the blank one to write down the name of a group for guided reading and the paper with the arrow to write down the name of the background group. The arrow points the background group to its work area.

Using the example below, you would ask the Whales to meet you at the reading table, the Sharks to meet as a background group, and everyone else to work on their color group assignment. (Write "Sharks" on the laminated 9 X 12 paper that has the arrow on it. The arrow leads the Sharks to their background group meeting area).

All three groups change approximately every 20 minutes. In one hour all students would have:

    1. Worked with a center or work assignment for 20 minutes
    2. Worked with a second center or work assignment for 20 minutes
    3. Worked with the teacher in a guided reading format or worked in a background group format for 20 minutes

You are now ready to begin implementing guided reading instruction because you have created a solid foundation for students working independently at centers or at their seats!

In this example there are:

      6 assignment groups
      5 guided reading groups

Students come from all different centers. Notice that you can start with five in a center because when you call for groups, the number of students that remain in the center drops by one or two.

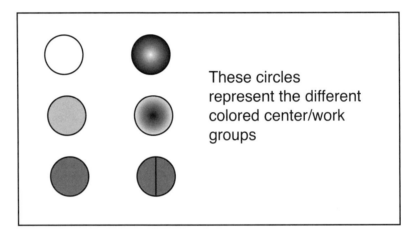

These circles represent the different colored center/work groups

S = Sharks

D = Dolphins

W = Whales

C = Clams

F = Fish

These letters represent the different guided reading groups.

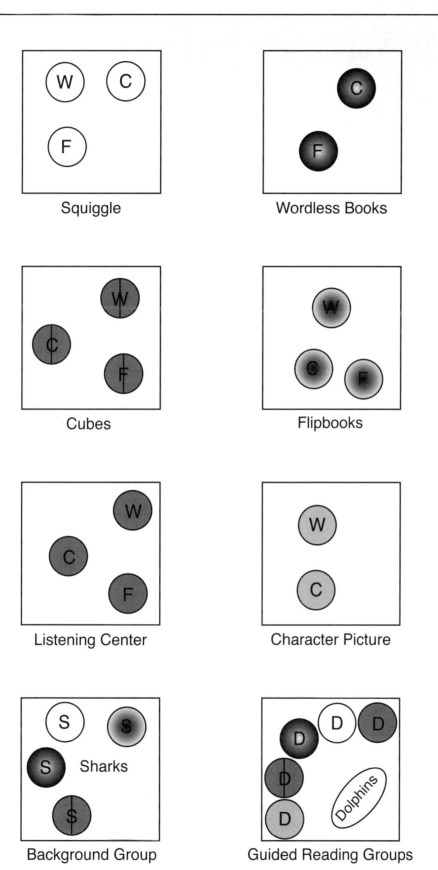

Squiggle

Wordless Books

Cubes

Flipbooks

Listening Center

Character Picture

Background Group

Sharks

Guided Reading Groups

Dolphins

OVERVIEW OF ACTIVITIES

Activity	Page	Changes made to the center	First Grade Examples	Second Grade Examples	Third Grade Examples	Fourth Grade Examples
Top Ten	64	topic for the list of ten items	things that are red	favorite foods	mammals	sentences with a simple subject
Picture Tales	70	new picture	choose a picture and write about it	⟶		↑
Squiggles	73	new squiggle	write about the new squiggle picture	⟶		↑
Character Pictures	77	new character picture	put the character into a picture and write about it	⟶		↑
Letters and Notes	79	name of person to write to	write to a classmate	write a thank you letter	write a business letter	write a letter to a historical figure
Journals	82	different topics	what I did at home last night	my pet	what I want to be when I grow up	a book review
Stackable Trays	82	different "fill-in" sheet	complete "fill-in"	⟶		↑
Wordless Books	83	different book	label pictures	write sentences about each page	write the text to the book	⟶
Authors	84	different topic	write a story	⟶		↑
Literary Friends	86	new literary friend	draw a picture and label	draw a picture and write at least three sentences	draw a picture and write a paragraph	write one to two paragraphs
Story Rewrites and Innovations	89	different book	writing based on book text	⟶		↑
Flipbooks	91	topic for the flipbook	first, next, then, last	different types of weather	parts of speech	chapter summaries, main idea, supporting details

OVERVIEW OF ACTIVITIES

Activity	Page	Changes made to the center	First Grade Examples	Second Grade Examples	Third Grade Examples	Fourth Grade Examples
Fun Facts	94	different topic	draw a picture and write facts	→	mini reports	→
Character Portraits	96	different character	work with a character from any book	→		→
Vocabulary Fun	98	different vocabulary words	work with vocabulary words	→		→
Playing with Words	100	different pattern	work with spelling and phonics curriculum	→		→
Pull-Throughs and Flip-Overs	104	different pattern	at	ark	able	suffixes and prefixes
Walking the Room	105	skills and examples to find	letters of the alphabet	sight words	plurals	parts of speech
Listening Station	106	different book and follow-up activities	draw the characters	write about the characters	compare and contrast you and a character	write two paragraphs on a topic of choice
Pocket Chart	108	different curriculum	rhyming words	long vowel sounds	making words plural	syllables and accents
I Can Use It	109	different curriculum	complete sentences	using punctuation	dialogue	similes and metaphors
Find It and Mark It	110	different words	find sight words	→	find skills	→
Write a Sentence	111	different page in book	Look at the _____	I found a _____, used as a _____.	use the dictionary	→
Going, Going, Gone Clay or Playdough Sand or Salt Trays	112	different words	Practice writing sight words	→	spelling and content area words	→

OVERVIEW OF ACTIVITIES

Activity	Page	Changes made to the center	First Grade Examples	Second Grade Examples	Third Grade Examples	Fourth Grade Examples
Plastic Letters Arty Words Create It	112	different words	Practice writing sight words	→	spelling and content area words	→
Sentence Cubes	114	no change	roll, write, draw	→	use blank cubes to make sentence longer	→
Newspaper Detectives	116	skills and examples to find	"r" words	contractions	fact or opinion	summarizing an article
Morning Message	117	different message and embedded skills	sight words	punctuation	"ing" ending	similes and metaphors
Mobiles	119	different topic or skill	colors	transportation	solid, liquid, gas	landforms
Find It in a Book	120	skills and examples to find	capital letters	quotations marks	verbs	conjunctions
Playing with Poems	121	different poem(s)	sight words	rhyming words	descriptive words	poetry forms
Compare and Contrast	122	different topics from the curriculum	two objects	plural rules	two characters	two books

Part 4

Appendix

ORGANIZING AND SCHEDULING
FIVE GUIDED READING GROUPS

Monday   Tuesday   Wednesday   Thursday   Friday

ORGANIZING AND SCHEDULING
FOUR GUIDED READING GROUPS

Monday   Tuesday   Wednesday   Thursday   Friday

ORGANIZING AND SCHEDULING
FOUR GUIDED READING GROUPS
WITH WHOLE GROUP INSTRUCTION

Monday	Tuesday	Wednesday	Thursday	Friday

Whole Group ↓

Whole Group ↓

ORGANIZING AND SCHEDULING
FOUR GUIDED READING GROUPS
WITH WHOLE GROUP INSTRUCTION

Monday	Tuesday	Wednesday	Thursday	Friday

Whole Group

Whole Group

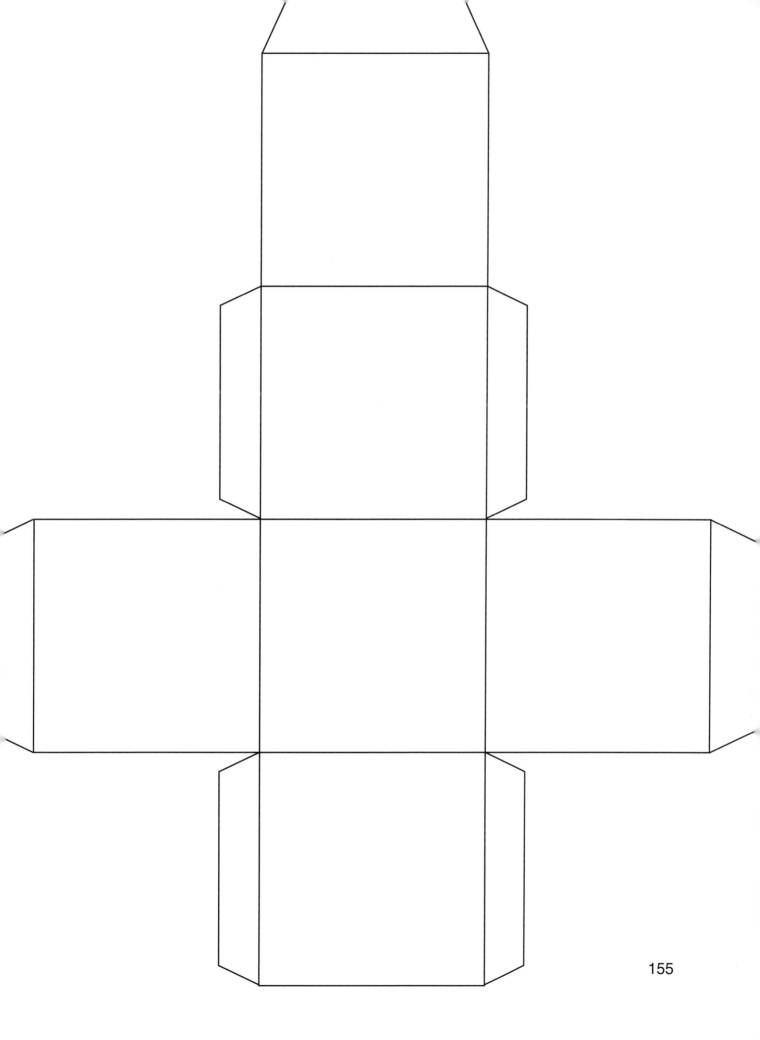

155

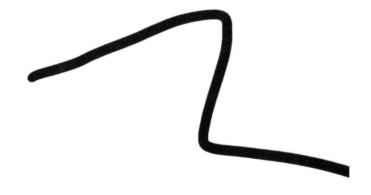

Name

Title of Article

Author

Fact	Opinion

Wordless Books

Title	Author
Alphabet City	Stephen Johnson
A Boy, a Dog and a Frog	Mercer Mayer
A Boy, a Dog, a Frog, and a Friend	Mercer Mayer
Changes Changes	Pat Hutchins
Deep in the Forest	Brinton Turkle
Dinosaur Day	Liza Donnelly
Eye Spy: A Book of Alphabet Puzzles	Linda Bourke
Flotsam	David Wiesner
Flowers for the Snowman	Gerda Marie Scheidl
Free Fall	David Wiesner
Frog on His Own	Mercer Mayer
Frog, Where Are You	Mercer Mayer
Good Dog, Carl (series)	Alexandra Day
Looking Down	Steve Jenkins
OOps	Arthur Geisert
Oink	Arthur Geisert
Pancakes for Breakfast	Tomie DePaola
Picnic	Emily McCully
Rain	Peter Spier
Sector 7	David Wiesner
The Chicken's Child	Margaret Hartelius
The Grey Lady and the Strawberry Snatcher	Molly Bang
The Mysteries of Harris Burdick	Chris Van Allsburg
The Red Book	Barbara Lehman
The Snowman	Raymond Briggs
Time Flies	Eric Rohmann
Tuesday	David Wiesner
We Hide, You Seek	Jose Aruego and Ariane Dewey
Why?	Nikolai Popov

Will's Mammoth?	Rafe Martin and Stephen Gammell
You Can't Take a Balloon Into The Metropolitan Museum	Jacqueline Preiss Weitzman and Robin Preiss Glasser
You Can't Take a Balloon Into The Museum of Fine Arts	Jacqueline Preiss Weitzman and Robin Preiss Glasser
Zoom	Istvan Banya

Parts of Speech Books by Ruth Heller

Title	**Skill**
A Cache of Jewels	Collective Nouns
Behind the Mask	Prepositions
Fantastic! Wow! and Unreal!	Interjections and Conjunctions
Kites Sail High	Verbs
Many Luscious Lollipops	Adjectives
Merry-Go-Round	Nouns
Mine, All Mine	Pronouns
Up, Up and Away	Adverbs

Poetry Books

Title	**Author**
Big, Bad and a Little Bit Scary	Wade Zahares
Boston Tea Party	Pamela Duncan Edwards
A Burst of Firsts	J. Patrick Lewis
I Invited a Dragon to Dinner	Chris L. Demarest
Readers' Theatre	Robyn Reeves, Laurence Swinburne, and Jack Warner
Paul Revere's Ride	Henry Wadsworth Longfellow
You Read to Me, I'll Read to You	Mary Ann Hoberman and Michael Emberley

Professional Reading and Resources

Boushey, Gail and Joan Moser. 2009. *The Café Book: Engaging All Students in Daily Literacy Assessment & Instruction*. Portland, Maine: Stenhouse Publishers.

Boyles, Nancy N. 2004. *Constructing Meaning through Kid-Friendly Comprehension Strategy Instruction*. Gainesville, Florida: Maupin House.

Davis, Judy and Sharon Hill. 2003. *The No-Nonsense Guide to Teaching Writing*. Portsmouth, New Hampshire: Heinemann.

Diller, Debbie. 2003. *Literacy Work Station: Making Centers Work*. Portland, Maine: Stenhouse Publishers.

Diller, Debbie. 2005. *Practice with Purpose: Literacy Stations for Grades 3-6*. Portland, Maine: Stenhouse Publishers.

Diller, Debbie. 2008. *Spaces & Places: Designing Classrooms for Literacy*. Portland, Maine: Stenhouse Publishers.

Fisher, Douglas and Nancy Frey. *Checking for Understanding: Formative Assessment Tecniques for Your Classroom*. Alexandria, Virginia: ASCD.

Forsten, Char and Jim Grant. 2002. *Differentiated Instruction: Different Strategies for Different Learners*. Peterborough, New Hampshire: Crystal Springs Books.

Harvey, Stephanie and Anne Goudvis. 2007. *Strategies That Work*. Portland, Maine: Stenhouse Publishers.

Hollas, Betty. 2005. *Differentiating Instruction in a Whole-Group Setting*. Peterborough, New Hampshire: Crystal Springs Books.

Johnson, Pat. 2006. *One Child at a Time: Making the Most of Your Time with Struggling Readers, K-6*. Portland, Maine: Stenhouse Publishers.

Hahn, Mary Lee. 2002. *Reconsidering Read-Aloud*. Portland, Maine: Stenhouse Publishers.

McEwan, Elaine K. 2004. *7 Strategies of Highly Effective Readers: Using Cognitive Research to Boost K-8 Achievement*. Thousand Oaks, California: Corwin Press.

Marzano, Robert J. 2006. *Classroom Assessment & Grading that Work*. Alexandria, Virginia: ASCD.

Marzano, Robert J. 2003. *What Works in Schools: Translating Research into Action*. Alexandria, Virginia: ASCD.

McLaughlin, Maureen and Glenn DeVoogd. *Critical Literacy: Enhancing Students' Comprehension of Text*. New York, New York: Scholastic.

Mere, Cathy. 2005. *More Than Guided Reading: Finding the Right Instructional Mix, K-3*. Portland, Maine: Stenhouse Publishers.

Miller, Debbie. 2002. *Reading with Meaning: Teaching Comprehension in the Primary Grades*. Portland, Maine: Stenhouse Publishers.

Sibberson, Franki and Karen Szymusiak. 2003. *Still Learning to Read: Teaching Students in Grades 3-6*. Portland, Maine: Stenhouse Publishers.

Stead, Tony. 2009. *Good Choice! Supporting Independent Reading and Response K-6*. Portland, Maine: Stenhouse Publishers.

Stewart, Margaret Taylor. 2002. *Writing "It's in the Bag:" Ways to Inspire Your Students to Write*. Peterborough, New Hampshire: Crystal Springs Books.

Szymusiak, Karen and Franki Sibberson. 2008. *Beyond Leveled Books: Supporting Early and Transitional Readers in Grades K-5*. Portland, Maine: Stenhouse Publishers.

Wilhelm, Jeffery PH.D. 2004. *Reading is Seeing*. New York, New York: Scholastic.

Notes

Notes

The illustrator, Patrick Vincent, is a graduate of Fairmont State University. He has been illustrating practically since birth. Whether it be movies, art, or writing, he is always creating something, often with unpredictable and spectacular results. A talented Graphic Designer, Patrick takes an idea and brings it to life. He resides in wild and wonderful West Virginia with his sweet chocolate lab, Miss Django.

Patrick's artwork, films, and writing can be viewed at: web.mac.com/patrick304

Patricia Pavelka presents dynamic workshops for teachers, administrators, and parents (grades K-8). To comment on this book, share your experiences and students' work, or reach Pat, please contact us at info@huskytrailpress.com (or write/fax to the addresses on the copyright page). Thank you.

 Husky Trail Press LLC is based on the courage, leadership, and loyalty of the Husky. The Husky's ability to always do its very best and excel, no matter how difficult the obstacles, is an encouragement to us.

Books Authored by Pat Pavelka

Differentiating Instruction
in a Whole-Group Setting
This book will show you how to bring differentiation into your whole-group classroom. Learn how to support those who need more time to grasp concepts, as well as challenge those who learn quickly. Grades 1-4. 160 pages. $20.95.

Question Prompts
This is a practical, use it in your classroom tomorrow, guide to help students to independently ask good, thought-provoking questions. This book contains specific prompts for the six question words and nonfiction. Specific ideas and activities for using the prompts are explained. Grades 1-8. 64 color pages. $14.95.

Squiggles
So Much Writing, So Much Fun, So Much Creativity
Helps students develop imaginations, poetry, and stories. Squiggles help differentiate assignments and can be used with students of all ability levels! Grades 1-8. 48 color pages. $12.95.

Cubes
Discussion Activities for Literacy and Skill Development
Teachers will liven up whole group discussions, mini-lessons, and small group interactions. Students will apply and utilize skills, not just memorize! Grades 1-8. 8 color pages plus inserts. $12.95.

Differentiated Assignments
This book demonstrates how to differentiate the daily assignments teachers give students. Teachers plan one activity that can be completed by students of different ability levels. Grades 1-8. Flip tab. 42 color pages. $12.95.

Create Independent Learners
Teacher-Tested Strategies for All Ability Levels
This book is full of ideas, strategies, and activities to help all ability-level students become independent learners. Grades 1-5. 160 pages. $19.95.

Making the Connection
Learning Skills Through Literature
Pat demonstrates how to move toward creating a literature-based reading program that actively involves students in learning. One book is for grades K-2 (136 pages) and one book is for grades 3-6 (144 pages). $19.95.

Foodle
Foodle is a fascinating fish with an "interesting" attribute. Children's book. Educational activities included. 32 color pages. $9.99.

The Adventures of Victor
Victor the Cat loved his life in the city, but moved to the country. Children's book. Educational activities. 32 color pages. $9.99.

CD $7.99 *and Cassette* $5.99.

w w w . h u s k y t r a i l p r e s s . c o m